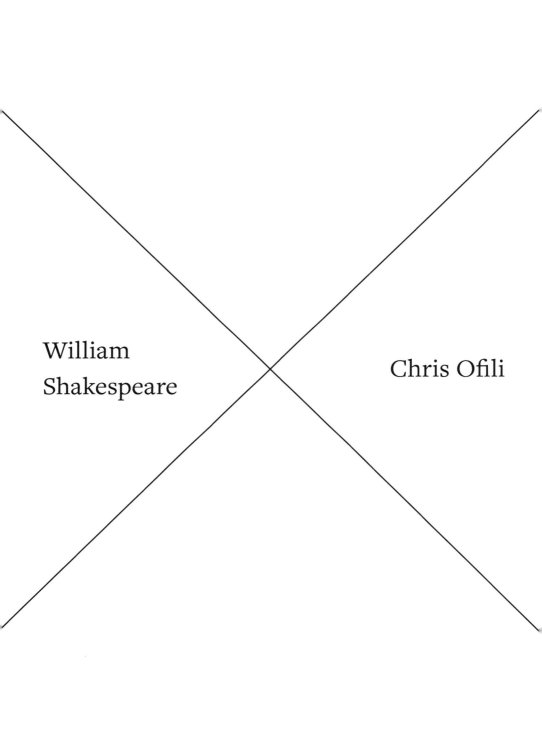

William
Shakespeare

Chris Ofili

The Tragedy of Othello
The Moor of Venice

By William Shakespeare
With an introduction by Fred Moten
Artwork by Chris Ofili

David Zwirner Books

Ofili's Othello

1

Though it is not usually characterized as such, Shakespeare's *Othello* is a "problem play," one doubly so. There's just enough carnival to render troubling its status as tragedy, despite the emphatic announcement of its full title, *The Tragedy of Othello, the Moor of Venice*. In the final chapter of his *Shakespeare's Festive World*, François Laroque excavates the festivity and festivities that undergird and undermine *Othello*'s darkness, showing how even the lyric richness of Othello's speech has an air of pestilent farce, just as the depth of his pain is rooted in and by Iago's brutal comic energy.[1] Moreover, that Othello is a moor of Venice means that the problem of the color line, which W. E. B. Du Bois locates in the twentieth century at its outset, is a problem of the centuries, whether we are talking about the seventeenth, twentieth, or twenty-first. And it's not so much that Shakespeare has given an early articulation of the Negro Problem; it's that, instead, he has given Negroes a problem. There's some shit we have to deal with in the wake of this play, a toxic atmosphere with which we must contend. The greatness of the play is not lessened by its being thus problematic; and this is because, rather than in spite, of how that greatness is bound up with the intense and gorgeous flatulence the play produces and gives off and plays with, its author slyly glancing at someone or other of us, asking, Did you cut that one? Often, as if in payment for the dis/honor of being so addressed, because look how good and how horrific it is to be addressed at all, we've taken responsibility for Shakespeare's ill wind, embracing it like a sail, or riding it like a wing, in the interest of some outward or upward mobility—which is to say, nobility—that it can only seize, not send. So that the terribly beautiful, evilly compounded genius of it is that what we are constrained to do with Othello when we enact him is act like him.

White fantasies of blackness underwrite both the play and its main character such that Othello's dignity, given in an insistence upon his dignity that renders him all but absolutely undignified, becomes the charge of a series of great black performers, from Ira Aldridge to Laurence Fishburne. Part of the respectability they would bring to and find in both character and play resides in their refusal to allow, from instance to instance in the more recent history of the play's production, the character to be portrayed by a white actor in blackface, particularly insofar as such an actor might succumb to the tempting imperative to reveal the Moor as dupe and as duplicitous. Tragedy ought not be let to fall into comic foolishness, especially when black folks and our dignity are involved, by way of the indignities of voluntary conscription. It's not that tragedy doesn't so fall from time to time in Shakespeare's oeuvre, whether in what folks are wont to call tragedy proper or in various comical or historical or comical-historical excursions into the realm of the tragic, as when Polonius breaks the law of genre when he would recite it, or in Hamlet's all but slapstick inability to act, or the silliness of Richard of Bordeaux's sadness; it's just that in those cases it is generally assumed to have nothing to do with us either in *Hamlet*'s or *Richard II*'s themes or casting, Shakespeare's invention of the human, there, being not but nothing other than his invention of whiteness, too. Isn't it absolutely appropriate, then, that a white actor should enact, and be thoughtfully responsible for, a white fantasy of blackness?[2] But that's just a black fantasy of whiteness and its mythic capabilities. Wherever and whenever we are, black performers of Othello can't simply allow him to be a lying fool like every other human subject. Interestingly, this is part of the logic driving an equally impressive line of black actors' refusal to embody the Moor that stretches from Sidney Poitier to Harry Lennix.[3] Either way, black folks are enjoined to take responsibility for white fantasy and solve a problem not of their own making.

2

Because he is so clearly in love with Othello, whose power to seduce is given in that he is impossible to love and not to love, Chris Ofili responds to him by beautifully and brilliantly declining to take responsibility for him. Because of this, Ofili's portraits of Othello, which somehow incorporate both performative enactment and nonperformative refusal, might open up new pathways in the history of Othello's portrayal. When we consider the double valence of the word "portray," as the act congeals into an artist's portrait or is dispersed in an actor's portrayal, things clear up in the blurring of the line between thing and event. What does it mean to portray Othello, where the beauty of the language of that role, or the depth of human feeling it bears, is still filtered through the protocols of blackface no matter who plays it. "One" who has never been conferred the status of one, in spite of having the imperative to be one mercilessly imposed upon "him," is compelled to search for, draw forth, extract, pluck out the mystery of a character who is, as Frantz Fanon would say, enslaved to his appearance. To portray is already to activate a range of rigorous attention to the presentation of the self which is not one, all across the sensual register of its surfaces, in the service of drawing or drawing out the mysterious depths of the inapparent. But what are the protocols for portraying a character who is always so clearly acting, so consciously performing, so emphatically disappearing? What is there in this role beyond oratorical expression, particularly insofar as it seems to have been devised to do nothing so much as constitute the occasion for that question? And how can the product of such devising be envisaged? Can Othello be given a face, or can his face be found, and saved, if that face is black or blackened? It is as if the role that instantiates the irreducible question concerning the superficiality of the "role" had to have been filtered through what Fanon calls "a racial epidermal schema."[4] Is there, or can there be, an experience of Othello that lies, as it were, underneath the surface that will have been Othello's occasion? Could such an experience transcend the limits of its occasion? Is there anything other than a lie lying beneath Othello's skin? How one might draw that, or draw that out, is a practical aesthetic question whose utterance, along with every other one of its procedures for solution, hides and presupposes the question concerning a violent ethics of extraction.

Is it right to marshal the forces of composition, improvisation, and interpretation to get at the soul of Othello? Of course, this surreptitious question bears and hides another: Does Othello, who is given as a function of surface given over to servility's enactment of nobility, have a soul? Does Shakespeare offer soul or a profound and problematic soullessness in Othello? And what does it mean when the one who is sent to find/extract that soul is constrained also to provide it? At stake is individuation's vacancy, which is different from its failure. What if the problem is not that Othello suffers (from) that impurity, of which Fanon writes, that infests or interdicts the worldview of the colonized but, rather, that he suffers from and in such impurity's absence? What if blackface is required to reveal this perfect vacuum, a poverty which, then, black actors are enjoined to alleviate whether they play Othello or not? Then, Othello is pursued while in the guise of the pursuer. Eloquent, reticent suit is his livery; his habit is given in the arrogant pride of every humble act of speech before the signiory, by whom he is insatiably wanted. 'Tis strange, 'tis passing strange, 'tis pitiful, 'tis wondrous pitiful, this unvarnished vanishing he undertakes if, in fact, there is no soul within Othello's house, which is his language. In this case, *Twelfth Night*'s Olivia is Othello's imperfect, anticipatory analogue; and this question of suit, pursuit, and merely seeming arises again, all the way down to the echoic oohs and ohs, like the babbling gossip of the air, which their hollow presences generate.[5] Remember how, in drag, Viola answers a question posed by Olivia, who would be wooed by her, about how she would be wooed by her? In response, Viola declares, while wooing Olivia on Orsino's behalf, a subjunctive intention to violate Olivia, the beloved of the one she serves, and loves, that she would:

> Make me a willow cabin at your gate
> And call upon my soul within the house.
> Write loyal cantons of contemned love
> And sing them loud even in the dead of night.
> Halloo your name to the reverberate hills
> And make the babbling gossip of the air
> Cry out "Olivia!" Oh, you should not rest
> Between the elements of air and earth,
> But you should pity me.[6]

Similarly, we are and would be pierced by the opulent confusion of air and wound in Othello's wooing. We are, along with Desdemona, enveloped in the penetrative depth of his sounding and, like her, are compelled to give, in return, a world of sighs, which Ofili converts to something visible in the curvaceous drawing and drawing out of his portrait. He who would portray Othello must so pursue that constantly unsatisfied suitor in order to attain the empty individuation they must share, expose, and so disperse. In this regard, "portray" carries "betray" like some extra baggage. This touches upon the tricky changing of suit to which Othello confesses when he relates the courtship of his bride. In telling the state the story of how he played his cards right with Desdemona, Othello—always cognizant of the need to regulate the way it wants him—plays, again, his cards right with the state; in narrating his pursuit of Desdemona, which consists of inducing her pursuit of him, Othello's consent is revealed as the demure function of his own design:

> These things to hear
> Would Desdemona seriously incline.
> But still the house affairs would draw her thence,
> Which ever as she could with haste dispatch
> She'd come again, and with a greedy ear
> Devour up my discourse. Which I, observing,
> Took once a pliant hour, and found good means
> To draw from her a prayer of earnest heart
> That I would all my pilgrimage dilate,
> Whereof by parcels she had something heard,
> But not intentively. I did consent,
> And often did beguile her of her tears
> When I did speak of some distressful stroke
> That my youth suffered. My story being done,
> She gave me for my pains a world of sighs.
> She swore, in faith, 'twas strange, 'twas passing strange,
> 'Twas pitiful, 'twas wondrous pitiful.
> She wished she had not heard it, yet she wished
> That heaven had made her such a man. She thanked me,
> And bade me, if I had a friend that loved her,
> I should but teach him how to tell my story,
> And that would woo her. Upon this hint I spake. (1.3.160–181)

Consider what it is to have drawn from the object of one's desire a prayer for one's own consent; consider the ethics of such mutual beguiling and pursuit in suited semblance, against the grain of any notion of suitability even in chaste ceremonies of talking and listening, which renders soul vulnerable, achievable in all her movement inside and outside the house, to the rhythm of all his soft-spoken breaking and entering; then, listen to the rich proliferation of "soul" in *Othello*'s first act and see if you can see if Othello has one, or any, even when, especially when, he declares his soul's perfection.

There's a constancy of inauthentic seeming that Othello is made to stand for. It is as if, on the one hand, he knows that he stands for it while, on the other hand, not knowing that he cannot know what he stands for. Iago is, in this regard, epiphenomenal, speaking of Othello that which Othello cannot speak. Rather, constrained to represent without knowing that what he represents is inauthenticity, Othello keeps saying that he is what he is while constantly showing that he is not. "But that I love the gentle Desdemona," Othello declares to Iago, his ancient id-like alter ego and projection, "I would not my unhousèd free condition/Put into circumscription and confine/For the sea's worth" (1.2.27–30). Love has demanded his dissimulation, and domesticated him, so that he can pursue and win his object, which is, in fact, that of and for which he both plays and is the object, a double operation that obliterates the separable integrity of its elements. The blurring of just being and just playing is their disappearance, and the impurity that remains, and which Othello enacts, and of which he is the enactment, is not something he can then claim as his own. He thinks he knows when he's just playing, and he thinks he knows when he's just being, but he never knows that when he's doing one he's always also doing the other and is, therefore, never doing either one. Being is not what it is but he's not even that. Othello seems, and serves his seeming up to others so they can devour it. He beguiles them into asking for a consent that, in any case, he could not have withheld. He seems to be a semiotic vector, a semantic event, a perfect flaw or fault through which the ethical pressure that accrues to a metaphysical mistake is released as the already given sexual and racial content of a murderous home. Sovereignty's forced, unforged performance couldn't be given more emphatically than in the tragic burlesque of blackface situation comedy.

3

Having been constrained and enticed to care for such a radically unlovable character; having been forced and gratified to bear the way he represents us; having been compelled and enabled to extract nobility from servility, then commonness from nobility, while recognizing in his blatant humility a general aspiration we are supposed to feel, and share: What does Ofili draw out of Othello? A set of variations on the forehead. What's inscribed there? Why is it inscribed? Who is Othello that he is or can be written on in this way? Is this an imposition of Ofili's or something he reveals, or redoubles, reveling in what is already given in Shakespeare? Does Ofili discover the real Othello or remask him? How to disclose the one who is not real, who is not one, who cannot be? Does etching enlighten or benight? Is there a truth now on the skin that in another way the skin had always hidden? Othello is an experiment in black personhood for which black persons are not responsible. Why did Fishburne take it on? Why did Lennix take it on by seeming to disavow it? How does Ofili now refuse it?

In offering us a classic mix of improvisation and revision, moving forward by looking back in wonder into the wreck of Othello's life, which is the disastrous chance he was never meant to survive, Ofili gifts Othello with a run of extravagant *bindis* meant to match the eighthead luxury of his forehead. Many peoples say the forehead is the point at which creation begins; this is more than simply an Athenian urge. Rather, a general mandala forms around some surrealistic spot, and energy is retained in Ofili's swift impromptus. His profligate lining out of the tragedy on Othello's head is an ornamental document of what's in Othello's head, which, then, Othello's face is constrained, serially, smilingly, to celebrate in tears.

Ofili's embroidery of Othello's visage, which Desdemona says she saw in Othello's mind, which sounds a whole new level of what seems, turns inscription into a kind of speech, a retelling of that prospective telling Othello invokes "of one whose subdued eyes,/ Albeit unused to the melting mood,/Drops tears as fast as the Arabian trees/Their medicinable gum" (5.2.396–399). That resin, when mixed with water, becomes varnish—tears thereby both marring and authenticating the tale Othello's face now tells in the rapid flow of Ofili's inscription, eroding the hard gloss of himself that Othello projects in impossible self-protection. Gloss's multiple edge is, in this regard, insistent: interpretation, as in some movement beneath the surface, combines with a hardening, decorative concealment of surface. There is a scratched-up luster, both extemporaneous and nonarbitrary, which Ofili reveals in redoubling Shakespeare's own redoubled revelation. Shakespeare creates a character for whom there is, and can be, no nonperformative moment. He imposes upon us a terrible gift that performs that imperative to perform, which somehow seems to be Othello's alone, which those of us who share it nonetheless are constrained to recognize.

To find something in Othello, then, requires digging, scratching, some elaborate corrosion of the corrosion of and to which Othello is subject. Othello's lyrical bellowing is supposed to countermand the general order of antiblackness that his blackness gives while bearing the general dissolution of the very idea of Europe even in his protection of it from "the general enemy Ottoman" (1.3.55). No servile service to the state could be more grand or futile; and the futility is revealed in the grandiosity, which is serial. Every staging, every production, every iteration is doomed to mar the portrait of sovereignty it projects and would protect. There's a kind of commerce between Othello and Falstaff in Verdi's late work that anticipates Ofili's moves along music's way, past portrayal and portraiture to some more general passing through, an operatic unworking of personality, its (dis)placement in passage, which, of course, Shakespeare pre-anticipates, his tragic figures always falling apart into something that feels almost atonal, the flipside being the comic social entanglement of the Eastcheap Ensemble. Verdi gets at that by way of a kind of chromaticism whose analogue on the face of Ofili's Othello is a crowdedness of line befitting an "extravagant and wheeling stranger/Of here and everywhere" (1.1.144–145).[7]

That's how those marks remark a way for black folks to worry Othello, within the terrible history of our having to worry about him. Ofili writes a subtle, (P)an-African, meta-Caribbean extension of what Aimé Césaire does through and with Caliban, what Kamau Brathwaite does to and for Sycorax, amplifying and embellishing, in pulling and pulling away from, the trigger of visibility.[8] Who is Othello's mother? Something of how she is purloined and

misconstrued is unsaid but seen in the inscription that disappears
her in the berries of her disappearing handkerchief. Where was
she taken? How will she be recovered? She is as quiet, too, as
Algerian danger, but Ofili's audiovisual stylus—not with engraving's
dot-matrixed burr but rather in more directly handed, looped
adornment—says something deep occurs when marking is also
sounding. In this regard, Ofili's all but phonographic sensitivity
lets us listen to obscurity and look at silence.

4

Ofili's Othello is festive through his tears, which ought not surprise
us since, again, Shakespeare's Othello is rife with festivity, Iago's
acidic clownishness corroding the ground upon which patriarchal
sovereignty should walk, since a state has to state in black and
white, like Adrienne Kennedy's movie star.[9] Ground is doubly at
stake in Ofili's etchings. The needle marks corrosion on the ground,
etching allowing the flow that engraving seizes, which brushstroke
thickens unto the line's plush unwieldiness. In these etchings, a
cursive discursivity ensues as mellifluous counterpart to Othello's
speech—which is his game—like a secondary rhythm. Ofili's Othello
is a weighty calypsonian, a fat man with the hard blues, to which
antiblackness corresponds in general but incompletely. And the
aphrodisiacal force of Othello's talk is so smooth that you can close
your eyes and almost hear him say, Come up and see my etchings.
He is, in this regard, like another old Shakespearean seducer who
spirits youth away from its proper, sovereign, patriarchal bonds. So
that the Falstaffian fleshiness Ofili brings to Othello's face in having
found it there already—the fullness he draws both to and from it—
is fitting even as it always threatens to exceed the compass of the
frame in an unhousèd freedom that is aligned with what Nathaniel
Mackey calls "unhoused vacuity."[10] That his flesh is inscribed
redoubles the fleshy inscription in which he's given in and by Ofili.
Like Falstaff, Othello is overblown, cartoonish, given to "giddy stilt."
He's a windbag, who let Iago, his invention, blow smoke up his ass.
Like Falstaff, Othello talks shit a mile a minute—talks way more
than he fights—and their resemblance asks us to consider whether

Othello's honor is anything other than hot air, as Falstaff intimates of honor more generally in the public/private staging of this soliloquy in *Henry IV, Part I*:

> What is honor? A word. What is in that word "honor"? What is that "honor"? Air. A trim reckoning. Who hath it? He that died o' Wednesday. Doth he feel it? No. Doth he hear it? No. 'Tis insensible, then? Yea, to the dead. But will it not live with the living? No. Why? Detraction will not suffer it. Therefore, I'll none of it. Honor is a mere scutcheon. And so ends my catechism.[11]

Ofili's Othello is a goodly, portly man, a corpulent, and this indicates a complex dis/possession of appetite, as if he were a rake all along, prone to some boastfully inadvertent owning up to his capacity to enchant given in immodest declaration of his modesty. His rap is so strong, in this regard, that it makes you wish Othello had been played by Isaac Hayes. What if the entire catalogue of Ike's Raps were a partially recovered edition of Othello's pre-*Othello* speeches, giving us an amplified glimpse of his address to the ladies?[12]

Of course, the difference between Othello and Falstaff is that Othello will have—or at least assert, both publicly and privately— his honor, which implies just that measure of self-deception that makes him serviceable for the state rather than essentially, even radically, useless to it. But what if Othello really did get down with Emilia? What if the one charged with portraying him were able to bring to and find in him the dissembler's shit-eating grin? What new portrayals do Ofili's imaginal portraits now make possible? Wouldn't it be amazing to see a black actor play Othello without being responsible for Othello? At least Falstaff is "a huge bombard of sack" rather than honor's empty vessel. Wouldn't it be cool, now that Black Moses[2] is gone, to see Danielle Brooks bring to and find in Othello's "bombast circumstance" all and more of what she found in and brought to Beatrice in the Public Theater's 2019 production of *Much Ado About Nothing*?[13] Her performance might carry out that triple negation that lets us know Othello ain't about nothing noway. Bringing the noise of a trace of something she might see, after all, in the pungent perfume with which Shakespeare fills his lungs would be her way of providing that flavor we feel, showing Othello and *Othello* some black, corrosive love. We hate the shit we have to deal with in that shit because we love that shit. Othello has us at hello. Ofili lets *Othello* go.

Notes

1   See François Laroque, *Shakespeare's Festive World: Elizabethan Seasonal Entertainment and the Professional Stage* (Cambridge: Cambridge University Press, 1991), pp. 282–302.

2   For an excellent discussion of black actors' consideration of whether or not Othello should be left to their white counterparts, see Ayanna Thompson, "The Blackfaced Bard: Returning to Shakespeare or Leaving Him?," *Shakespeare Bulletin* (Fall 2009), pp. 437–456. Along with Laroque's great book, I have been greatly informed and influenced by Thompson's article, and by the rest of the work she gathers and edits in this special issue, and by her work in general.

3   The challenging and rewarding problem that Shakespeare and his industry generally poses for black actors is powerfully addressed by Fishburne and Lennix in "Two Actors on Shakespeare, Race, and Performance: A Conversation Between Harry J. Lennix and Laurence Fishburne," *Shakespeare Bulletin* (Fall 2009), pp. 399–414.

4   Frantz Fanon, *Black Skin, White Masks*, trans. Charles Lam Markmann (London: Pluto Press, 2008), p. 84.

5   See Joel Fineman, "The Sound of O in Othello: The Real of the Tragedy of Desire," *October* (Summer 1988), pp. 76–96.

6   William Shakespeare, *Twelfth Night, or What You Will*, in William Shakespeare, *The Complete Works*, ed. Stanley Wells and Gary Taylor (Oxford: Clarendon Press, 1988), 1.5.257–265.

7   All I can do is gesture at what P. A. Skantze brilliantly elaborates, in her writing and in her stagecraft, on the possibilities of Shakespeare's operatic staging. Here, I am thinking of her "Addressing Opera: Putting the 'Lex' in Lexiturgy" (unpublished manuscript, May 14, 2019).

8   See Aimé Césaire, *Une tempête* (Paris: Éditions du Seuil, 1969); and Kamau Brathwaite, *Barabajan Poems: 1492–1992* (New York and Kingston: Savacou North, 1994).

9   See Adrienne Kennedy, "A Movie Star Has to Star in Black and White," in *In One Act* (Minneapolis: University of Minnesota Press, 1988), pp. 79–103.

10   Nathaniel Mackey, *From a Broken Bottle Traces of Perfume Still Emanate: Atet A.D.* (San Francisco: City Lights Books, 2001), p. 118.

11   William Shakespeare, *The History of Henry IV (1 Henry IV)*, in *The Complete Works*, 5.1.133–140.

12   Listen, for instance, to his "Ike's Rap 1," *To Be Continued*, Enterprise ENS-1014, 1970, LP; and, especially, to its unnumbered precursor, "I Stand Accused," *The Isaac Hayes Movement*, Enterprise ENS-1010, 1970, LP.

13   See Isaac Hayes, *Black Moses*, Enterprise ENS-5003, 1971, LP.

Othello

Characters in the play

OTHELLO, the Moor

BRABANTIO, father to Desdemona

DESDEMONA, wife to Othello

IAGO, a villain

EMILIA, wife to Iago

RODERIGO, a gulled gentleman

DUKE OF VENICE

MONTANO, Governor of Cyprus

CASSIO, a lieutenant

BIANCA, a courtesan

LODOVICO and GRATIANO, two noble Venetians

SENATORS

GENTLEMEN OF CYPRUS

SAILORS

CLOWN

SERVANTS, ATTENDANTS, OFFICERS, MESSENGERS,
HERALD, MUSICIANS, TORCHBEARERS

Act 1.

Scene 1.
A street in Venice

[Enter Roderigo and Iago.]

RODERIGO   Tush! Never tell me! I take it much unkindly
That thou, Iago, who hast had my purse
As if the strings were thine, shouldst know of this.

IAGO   S'blood, but you'll not hear me!
5   If ever I did dream of such a matter,
Abhor me.

RODERIGO   Thou toldst me thou didst hold him in thy hate.

IAGO   Despise me
If I do not. Three great ones of the city,
10   In personal suit to make me his lieutenant,
Off-capped* to him; and, by the faith of man,   *Took off their hats*
I know my price, I am worth no worse a place.
But he, as loving his own pride and purposes,
Evades them with a bombast circumstance,
15   Horribly stuffed with epithets of war;*   *military jargon*
And in conclusion,
Nonsuits* my mediators. For "Certes,"* says he,   *Denies | Certainly*
"I have already chose my officer."
And what was he?*   *(Othello)*
20   Forsooth,* a great arithmetician,   *In truth*
One Michael Cassio, a Florentine,
A fellow almost damned in a fair wife,
That never set a squadron in the field,
Nor the division* of a battle* knows   *ordering | troops*
25   More than a spinster*—unless the bookish theoric,*   *housewife | theory*
Wherein the tonguèd consuls can propose*   *talk*
As masterly as he. Mere prattle without practice

Is all his soldiership. But he, sir, had th' election;
And I, of whom his eyes had seen the proof
30 At Rhodes, at Cyprus, and on other grounds
Christened and heathen, must be beleed* and calmed   *cut off from*
By debitor and creditor. This countercaster,
He, in good time, must his lieutenant be,
And I, God bless the mark, his Moorship's ancient.*   *ensign*

35 RODERIGO   By heaven, I rather would have been his hangman.

IAGO   Why, there's no remedy. 'Tis the curse of service.
Preferment goes by letter and affection,
And not by old gradation,* where each second   *seniority*
Stood heir to th' first. Now, sir, be judge yourself
40 Whether I in any just term am affined*   *bound*
To love the Moor.

RODERIGO   I would not follow him, then.

IAGO   O, sir, content you.
I follow him to serve my turn upon him.*   *serve my own interests*
45 We cannot all be masters, nor all masters
Cannot be truly followed. You shall mark
Many a duteous and knee-crooking* knave   *bowing*
That, doting on his own obsequious bondage,
Wears out his time, much like his master's ass,
50 For naught but provender,* and when he's old, cashiered.*   *animal feed | discarded*
Whip me* such honest knaves! Others there are   *I'd have whipped*
Who, trimmed* in forms and visages of duty,   *dressed*
Keep yet their hearts attending on themselves,
And, throwing but shows of service on their lords,
55 Do well thrive by them; and when they have lined their coats,
Do themselves homage. These fellows have some soul,
And such a one do I profess myself. For, sir,
It is as sure as you are Roderigo,
Were I the Moor I would not be Iago.
60 In following him, I follow but myself.
Heaven is my judge, not I for* love and duty,   *not out of*

But seeming so for my peculiar* end.   *personal
For when my outward action doth demonstrate
The native act and figure of my heart
65 In complement extern,* 'tis not long after   *external appearance
But I will wear my heart upon my sleeve
For daws* to peck at. I am not what I am.   *crow-like birds

RODERIGO   What a full fortune does the thicklips owe*   *own
If he can carry 't thus!

70 IAGO   Call up her* father.   *(Desdemona's)
Rouse him. Make after him, poison his delight,
Proclaim* him in the streets; incense her kinsmen,   *Accuse
And, though he in a fertile climate dwell,
Plague him with flies. Though that his joy be joy,
75 Yet throw such chances of vexation on 't
As it may lose some color.*   *(basis)

RODERIGO   Here is her father's house. I'll call aloud.

IAGO   Do, with like timorous accent* and dire yell   *tone
As when, by night and negligence, the fire
80 Is spied in populous cities.

RODERIGO   What ho, Brabantio! Signior Brabantio, ho!

IAGO   Awake! What ho, Brabantio! Thieves, thieves!
Look to your house, your daughter, and your bags!*   *money bags
Thieves, thieves!

[*Enter Brabantio, above.*]

85 BRABANTIO   What is the reason of this terrible summons?
What is the matter there?

RODERIGO   Signior, is all your family within?

IAGO   Are your doors locked?

BRABANTIO   Why, wherefore ask you this?

90   IAGO   Zounds, sir, you're robbed. For shame, put on your gown!
Your heart is burst. You have lost half your soul.
Even now, now, very now, an old black ram
Is tupping* your white ewe. Arise, arise!   *copulating with*
Awake the snorting* citizens with the bell,   *snoring*
95   Or else the devil will make a grandsire of you.
Arise, I say!

BRABANTIO   What, have you lost your wits?

RODERIGO   Most reverend signior, do you know my voice?

BRABANTIO   Not I. What are you?

100   RODERIGO   My name is Roderigo.

BRABANTIO   The worser welcome.
I have charged thee not to haunt about my doors.
In honest plainness thou hast heard me say
My daughter is not for thee. And now in madness,
105   Being full of supper and distemp'ring draughts,*   *intoxicating drinks*
Upon malicious bravery dost thou come
To start* my quiet.   *disrupt*

RODERIGO   Sir, sir, sir—

BRABANTIO   But thou must needs be sure
110   My spirits and my place* have in their power   *rank*
To make this bitter to thee.

RODERIGO   Patience, good sir.

BRABANTIO   What tell'st thou me of robbing?
This is Venice. My house is not a grange.*   *country house*

115   RODERIGO   Most grave Brabantio,
In simple and pure soul I come to you—

IAGO   Zounds, sir, you are one of those that will not serve God if the
devil bid you. Because we come to do you service and you think we are
ruffians you'll have your daughter covered with a Barbary horse;*   *coupled with an animal
120 you'll have your nephews* neigh to you; you'll have coursers for   *grandsons
cousins and jennets for germans.*   *horses for relatives

BRABANTIO   What profane wretch art thou?

IAGO   I am one, sir, that comes to tell you your daughter and
the Moor are now making the beast with two backs.*   *copulating

125 BRABANTIO   Thou art a villain!

IAGO   You are a senator.

BRABANTIO   This thou shalt answer. I know thee, Roderigo.

RODERIGO   Sir, I will answer anything. But I beseech you,
If 't be your pleasure and most wise consent—
130 As partly I find it is—that your fair daughter,
At this odd even* and dull* watch o' th' night,   *near midnight / sleeping
Transported with no worse nor better guard
But with a knave of common hire, a gondolier,
To the gross clasps of a lascivious Moor:
135 If this be known to you, and your allowance,*   *allowed by you
We then have done you bold and saucy* wrongs.   *impudent
But if you know not this, my manners tell me
We have your wrong rebuke. Do not believe
That from* the sense of all civility   *contrary to
140 I thus would play and trifle with your Reverence.
Your daughter, if you have not given her leave,
I say again, hath made a gross revolt,
Tying her duty, beauty, wit, and fortunes
In an extravagant and wheeling* stranger   *restless
145 Of here and everywhere. Straight satisfy* yourself.   *Immediately inform
If she be in her chamber or your house,
Let loose on me the justice of the state
For thus deluding you.

BRABANTIO   Strike on the tinder,* ho!   *a light*
150 Give me a taper.* Call up all my people.   *candle*
This accident* is not unlike my dream.   *event*
Belief of it oppresses me already.
Light, I say, light!   [*He exits.*]

IAGO   [*to Roderigo*] Farewell, for I must leave you.
155 It seems not meet* nor wholesome to my place   *proper*
To be producted,* as if I stay I shall,   *brought forward as witness*
Against the Moor. For I do know the state,
However this may gall him with some check,*   *reprimand*
Cannot with safety cast* him, for he's embarked   *dismiss*
160 With such loud reason to the Cyprus wars,
Which even now stands in act, that, for their souls,
Another of his fathom* they have none   *capacity*
To lead their business. In which regard,
Though I do hate him as I do hell pains,
165 Yet, for necessity of present life,*   *livelihood*
I must show out a flag and sign of love—
Which is indeed but sign. That you shall surely find him,
Lead to the Sagittary the raisèd search,*   *awakened search party*
And there will I be with him. So, farewell.   [*He exits.*]

[*Enter Brabantio in his nightgown, with Servants and torches.*]

170 BRABANTIO   It is too true an evil. Gone she is,
And what's to come of my despisèd time*   *lifetime*
Is naught but bitterness.—Now, Roderigo,
Where didst thou see her?—O, unhappy girl!—
With the Moor, sayst thou?—Who would be a father?—
175 How didst thou know 'twas she?—O, she deceives me
Past thought!—What said she to you?—Get more tapers.
Raise all my kindred.—Are they married, think you?

RODERIGO   Truly, I think they are.

BRABANTIO   O heaven! How got she out? O treason of the blood!
180 Fathers, from hence trust not your daughters' minds

By what you see them act.—Is there not charms
By which the property* of youth and maidhood*   *nature / virginity*
May be abused? Have you not read, Roderigo,
Of some such thing?

185   RODERIGO   Yes, sir, I have indeed.

BRABANTIO   Call up my brother.—O, would you had had her!—
Some one way, some another.—Do you know
Where we may apprehend her and the Moor?

RODERIGO   I think I can discover him, if you please
190   To get good guard and go along with me.

BRABANTIO   Pray you lead on. At every house I'll call.
I may command* at most.*—Get weapons, ho!   *get help / most of them*
And raise some special officers of night.—
On, good Roderigo. I will deserve* your pains.   *reward*

[*They exit.*]

Scene 2.
Another street in Venice

[*Enter Othello, Iago, Attendants, with torches.*]

IAGO   Though in the trade of war I have slain men,
Yet do I hold it very stuff o' th' conscience
To do no contrived* murder. I lack iniquity   *premeditated*
Sometimes to do me service. Nine or ten times
5 I had thought t' have yerked* him here under the ribs.   *struck; attacked*

OTHELLO   'Tis better as it is.

IAGO   Nay, but he prated
And spoke such scurvy and provoking terms
Against your Honor,
10 That with the little godliness I have
I did full hard forbear him.* But I pray you, sir,   *restrained myself*
Are you fast married? Be assured of this,
That the magnifico* is much beloved,   *magistrate (Brabantio)*
And hath in his effect a voice potential*   *powerful*
15 As double as the Duke's. He will divorce you
Or put upon you what restraint or grievance
The law (with all his might to enforce it on)
Will give him cable.*   *scope*

OTHELLO   Let him do his spite.
20 My services which I have done the signiory*   *Venetian government*
Shall out-tongue his complaints. 'Tis yet to know*   *not yet known*
(Which, when I know that boasting is an honor,
I shall promulgate) I fetch my life and being
From men of royal siege,* and my demerits*   *rank / merits*
25 May speak unbonneted to as proud a fortune
As this that I have reached. For know, Iago,
But that I love the gentle Desdemona,

I would not my unhousèd* free condition   *unconfined*
Put into circumscription and confine
30 For the sea's worth. But look, what lights come yond?

IAGO   Those are the raisèd father and his friends.
You were best go in.

OTHELLO   Not I. I must be found.
My parts,* my title, and my perfect* soul   *qualities / clean; guiltless*
35 Shall manifest me rightly. Is it they?

IAGO   By Janus, I think no.

[*Enter Cassio, with Officers, and torches.*]

OTHELLO   The servants of the Duke and my lieutenant!
The goodness of the night upon you, friends.
What is the news?

40 CASSIO   The Duke does greet you, general,
And he requires your haste-post-haste appearance,
Even on the instant.

OTHELLO   What is the matter, think you?

CASSIO   Something from Cyprus, as I may divine.
45 It is a business of some heat.* The galleys   *urgency*
Have sent a dozen sequent* messengers   *successive*
This very night at one another's heels,
And many of the Consuls, raised and met,
Are at the Duke's already. You have been hotly called for.
50 When, being not at your lodging to be found,
The Senate hath sent about three several* quests   *separate*
To search you out.

OTHELLO   'Tis well I am found by you.
I will but spend a word here in the house
55 And go with you.   [*He exits.*]

CASSIO   Ancient, what makes he here?

IAGO   Faith, he tonight hath boarded a land carrack.*   *merchant ship*
If it prove lawful prize,* he's made forever.   *booty*

CASSIO   I do not understand.

60   IAGO   He's married.

CASSIO   To who?

IAGO   Marry,* to—   *Indeed; by Mary*
[*Reenter Othello.*]
                    Come, captain, will you go?

OTHELLO   Have with you.*   *Let's go*

65   CASSIO   Here comes another troop to seek for you.

[*Enter Brabantio, Roderigo, with Officers, and torches.*]

IAGO   It is Brabantio. General, be advised,
He comes to bad intent.

OTHELLO   Holla, stand there!

RODERIGO   Signior, it is the Moor.

70   BRABANTIO   Down with him, thief!

[*They draw their swords.*]

IAGO   You, Roderigo! Come, sir, I am for you.

OTHELLO   Keep up* your bright swords, for the dew will rust them   *Put away*
Good signior, you shall more command with years
Than with your weapons.

BRABANTIO   O, thou foul thief, where hast thou stowed my daughter?
75   Damned as thou art, thou hast enchanted her!
For I'll refer me* to all things of sense,*   *my case | rational beings*
If she in chains of magic were not bound,
Whether a maid so tender, fair, and happy,
80   So opposite to marriage that she shunned
The wealthy curlèd darlings of our nation,
Would ever have, t' incur a general mock,*   *mockery*
Run from her guardage to the sooty bosom
Of such a thing as thou—to fear, not to delight!
85   Judge me the world, if 'tis not gross in sense*   *obvious*
That thou hast practiced on* her with foul charms,   *tricked*
Abused her delicate youth with drugs or minerals
That weakens motion.* I'll have 't disputed on.*   *inclination | argued in court*
'Tis probable, and palpable to thinking.
90   I therefore apprehend and do attach* thee   *arrest*
For an abuser of the world, a practicer
Of arts inhibited and out of warrant.*—   *illegal*
Lay hold upon him. If he do resist,
Subdue him at his peril.

95   OTHELLO   Hold your hands,
Both you of my inclining* and the rest.   *following*
Were it my cue to fight, I should have known it
Without a prompter.—Whither will you that I go
To answer this your charge?

100   BRABANTIO   To prison, till fit time
Of law and course of direct session*   *next court session*
Call thee to answer.

OTHELLO   What if I do obey?
How may the Duke be therewith satisfied,
105   Whose messengers are here about my side,
Upon some present business of the state,
To bring me to him?

OFFICER   'Tis true, most worthy signior.
The Duke's in council, and your noble self
110   I am sure is sent for.

BRABANTIO   How? The Duke in council?
In this time of the night? Bring him away;
Mine's not an idle cause. The Duke himself,
Or any of my brothers of the state,
115   Cannot but feel this wrong as 'twere their own.
For if such actions may have passage free,
Bondslaves and pagans shall our statesmen be.

[*They exit.*]

Scene 3.
A Venetian council room

[*Enter the Duke, Senators, and Officers.*]

DUKE   There's no composition in this news
That gives them credit.

FIRST SENATOR   Indeed, they are disproportioned.*   *inconsistent*
My letters say a hundred and seven galleys.

5   DUKE   And mine, a hundred forty.

SECOND SENATOR   And mine, two hundred.
But though they jump not on a just account*   *don't agree*
(As in these cases, where the aim reports*   *estimates*
'Tis oft with difference), yet do they all confirm
10   A Turkish fleet, and bearing up to Cyprus.

DUKE   Nay, it is possible enough to judgment.
I do not so secure me in the error,
But the main article I do approve*   *believe*
In fearful sense.

15   SAILOR   [*within*] What ho, what ho, what ho!

[*Enter a Sailor.*]

OFFICER   A messenger from the galleys.

DUKE   Now, what's the business?

SAILOR   The Turkish preparation* makes for Rhodes.   *fleet ready for war*
So was I bid report here to the state
20   By Signior Angelo.   [*He exits.*]

DUKE   How say you by this change?

FIRST SENATOR   This cannot be,
By no assay* of reason. 'Tis a pageant   *test*
To keep us in false gaze. When we consider
25 Th' importancy of Cyprus to the Turk,
And let ourselves again but understand
That, as it more concerns the Turk than Rhodes,
So may he with more facile question bear it,
For that it stands not in such warlike brace,
30 But altogether lacks th' abilities
That Rhodes is dressed in*—if we make thought of this,   *equipped with*
We must not think the Turk is so unskillful
To leave that latest* which concerns him first,   *last*
Neglecting an attempt of ease and gain
35 To wake and wage a danger profitless.

DUKE   Nay, in all confidence, he's not for Rhodes.

OFFICER   Here is more news.

[*Enter a Messenger.*]

MESSENGER   The Ottomites,* Reverend and Gracious,*   *Turks / (to the Duke)*
Steering with due course toward the isle of Rhodes,
40 Have there injointed* them with an after* fleet.   *joined / another*

FIRST SENATOR   Ay, so I thought. How many, as you guess?

MESSENGER   Of thirty sail; and now they do restem*   *retrace*
Their backward course, bearing with frank appearance
Their purposes toward Cyprus. Signior Montano,
45 Your trusty and most valiant servitor,
With his free duty recommends* you thus,   *informs*
And prays you to believe him.

DUKE   'Tis certain, then, for Cyprus.
Marcus Luccicos, is not he in town?

50 FIRST SENATOR   He's now in Florence.

DUKE   Write from us to him.
Post-post-haste. Dispatch.

FIRST SENATOR   Here comes Brabantio and the valiant Moor.

[*Enter Brabantio, Othello, Cassio, Iago, Roderigo, and Officers.*]

DUKE   Valiant Othello, we must straight* employ you   *immediately*
55 Against the general enemy* Ottoman.   *of Christendom*
[*To Brabantio*] I did not see you. Welcome, gentle* signior.   *noble*
We lacked your counsel and your help tonight.

BRABANTIO   So did I yours. Good your Grace, pardon me.
Neither my place* nor aught* I heard of business   *official position | anything*
60 Hath raised me from my bed, nor doth the general care
Take hold on me, for my particular grief
Is of so floodgate and o'erbearing nature
That it engluts* and swallows other sorrows   *gulps*
And it is still itself.

65 DUKE   Why, what's the matter?

BRABANTIO   My daughter! O, my daughter!

FIRST SENATOR   Dead?

BRABANTIO   Ay, to me.
She is abused,* stol'n from me, and corrupted   *deceived*
70 By spells and medicines bought of mountebanks;*   *quacks*
For nature so prepost'rously to err—
Being not deficient, blind, or lame of sense—
Sans* witchcraft could not.   *Without*

DUKE   Whoe'er he be that in this foul proceeding
75 Hath thus beguiled your daughter of herself
And you of her, the bloody book of law

You shall yourself read in the bitter letter,
After your own sense, yea, though our proper* son   *own*
Stood in your action.*   *were charged*

80 BRABANTIO   Humbly I thank your Grace.
Here is the man—this Moor, whom now it seems
Your special mandate for the state affairs
Hath hither brought.

ALL   We are very sorry for 't.

85 DUKE   [*to Othello*] What, in your own part, can you say to this?

BRABANTIO   Nothing, but this is so.

OTHELLO   Most potent, grave, and reverend signiors,
My very noble and approved* good masters: *proven*
That I have ta'en away this old man's daughter,
90 It is most true; true I have married her.
The very head and front* of my offending   *chief*
Hath this extent, no more. Rude* am I in my speech,   *Unpolished*
And little blessed with the soft phrase of peace;
For since these arms of mine had seven years' pith,*   *strength*
95 Till now some nine moons wasted,* they have used   *nine months ago*
Their dearest* action in the tented field,*   *most valued | battlefield*
And little of this great world can I speak
More than pertains to feats of broils and battle.
And therefore little shall I grace my cause
100 In speaking for myself. Yet, by your gracious patience,
I will a round* unvarnished tale deliver   *direct*
Of my whole course of love—what drugs, what charms,
What conjuration, and what mighty magic
(For such proceeding I am charged withal)
105 I won his daughter.

BRABANTIO   A maiden never bold,
Of spirit so still and quiet that her motion
Blushed at herself. And she, in spite of nature,

Of years, of country, credit,* everything,   *reputation*

110 To fall in love with what she feared to look on!
It is a judgment maimed and most imperfect
That will confess perfection so could err
Against all rules of nature, and must* be driven   *we must*
To find out practices of cunning hell

115 Why this should be. I therefore vouch again
That with some mixtures powerful o'er the blood,*   *passions*
Or with some dram conjured* to this effect,   *magical dose*
He wrought upon her.

DUKE   To vouch this is no proof

120 Without more wider and more overt test*   *evidence*
Than these thin habits* and poor likelihoods   *conjecture*
Of modern seeming do prefer against him.

FIRST SENATOR   But, Othello, speak:
Did you by indirect and forcèd courses*   *means*

125 Subdue and poison this young maid's affections?
Or came it by request, and such fair question*   *conversation*
As soul to soul affordeth?

OTHELLO   I do beseech you,
Send for the lady to the Sagittary

130 And let her speak of me before her father.
If you do find me foul in her report,
The trust, the office I do hold of you,
Not only take away, but let your sentence
Even fall upon my life.

135 DUKE   Fetch Desdemona hither.

OTHELLO   Ancient, conduct them. You best know the place.
[*Iago and Attendants exit.*]
And till she come, as truly as to heaven
I do confess the vices of my blood,*   *sins of passion*
So justly to your grave ears I'll present

140 How I did thrive in this fair lady's love,
And she in mine.

DUKE   Say it, Othello.

OTHELLO   Her father loved me, oft invited me,
Still* questioned me the story of my life   *Constantly*
145   From year to year—the battles, sieges, fortunes
That I have passed.
I ran it through, even from my boyish days
To th' very moment that he bade me tell it,
Wherein I spoke of most disastrous chances:
150   Of moving accidents* by flood and field,   *events*
Of hairbreadth 'scapes i' th' imminent deadly breach,
Of being taken by the insolent foe
And sold to slavery, of my redemption thence,
And portance* in my traveler's history,   *conduct*
155   Wherein of antres* vast and deserts idle,   *caves*
Rough quarries, rocks, and hills whose heads touch heaven,
It was my hint* to speak—such was my process*—   *occasion | story*
And of the cannibals that each other eat,
The Anthropophagi, and men whose heads
160   Grew beneath their shoulders. These things to hear
Would Desdemona seriously incline.
But still the house affairs would draw her thence,
Which ever as she could with haste dispatch
She'd come again, and with a greedy ear
165   Devour up my discourse. Which I, observing,
Took once a pliant hour, and found good means
To draw from her a prayer of earnest heart
That I would all my pilgrimage dilate,*   *describe in detail*
Whereof by parcels she had something heard,
170   But not intentively. I did consent,
And often did beguile her of her tears
When I did speak of some distressful stroke
That my youth suffered. My story being done,
She gave me for my pains a world of sighs.
175   She swore, in faith, 'twas strange, 'twas passing strange,
'Twas pitiful, 'twas wondrous pitiful.
She wished she had not heard it, yet she wished
That heaven had made her such a man. She thanked me,

And bade me, if I had a friend that loved her,
180 I should but teach him how to tell my story,
And that would woo her. Upon this hint* I spake.   *opportunity
She loved me for the dangers I had passed,
And I loved her that she did pity them.
This only is the witchcraft I have used.
185 Here comes the lady. Let her witness it.

[*Enter Desdemona, Iago, and Attendants.*]

DUKE   I think this tale would win my daughter, too.
Good Brabantio,
Take up this mangled matter at the best.*   *best you can
Men do their broken weapons rather use
190 Than their bare hands.

BRABANTIO   I pray you hear her speak.
If she confess that she was half the wooer,
Destruction* on my head if my bad blame   *Let destruction fall
Light on the man.—Come hither, gentle mistress.
195 Do you perceive in all this noble company
Where most you owe obedience?

DESDEMONA   My noble father,
I do perceive here a divided duty.
To you I am bound for life and education.
200 My life and education both do learn* me   *teach
How to respect you. You are the lord of duty.
I am hitherto your daughter. But here's my husband.
And so much duty as my mother showed
To you, preferring you before her father,
205 So much I challenge* that I may profess   *assert
Due to the Moor my lord.

BRABANTIO   God be with you! I have done.
Please it your Grace, on to the state affairs.
I had rather to adopt a child than get* it.—   *father
210 Come hither, Moor.
I here do give thee that with all my heart

Which, but thou hast already, with all my heart
I would keep from thee.—For your sake, jewel,
I am glad at soul I have no other child,
215 For thy escape would teach me tyranny,
To hang clogs* on them.—I have done, my lord.   *weights

DUKE   Let me speak like yourself and lay a sentence,*   *employ a moral
Which as a grece* or step may help these lovers   *flight of stairs
Into your favor.
220 When remedies are past, the griefs are ended
By seeing the worst, which late on hopes depended.
To mourn a mischief* that is past and gone   *misfortune
Is the next way to draw new mischief on.
What cannot be preserved when fortune takes,
225 Patience her injury a mock'ry makes.
The robbed that smiles steals something from the thief;
He robs himself that spends a bootless* grief.   *pointless

BRABANTIO   So let the Turk of Cyprus us beguile,
We lose it not so long as we can smile.
230 He bears the sentence* well that nothing bears   *saying
But the free comfort which from thence he hears;
But he bears both the sentence and the sorrow
That, to pay grief, must of poor patience borrow.
These sentences to sugar or to gall,*   *bitter
235 Being strong on both sides, are equivocal.
But words are words. I never yet did hear
That the bruised heart was piercèd* through the ear.   *surgically lanced
I humbly beseech you, proceed to th' affairs of state.

DUKE   The Turk with a most mighty preparation makes for Cyprus.
240 Othello, the fortitude* of the place is best known to you. And though   *strength
we have there a substitute of most allowed sufficiency,* yet opinion,   *known ability
a sovereign mistress of effects, throws a more safer voice on you. You
must therefore be content to slubber* the gloss of your new fortunes   *stain
with this more stubborn* and boist'rous expedition.   *rougher

245 OTHELLO   The tyrant custom, most grave senators,
Hath made the flinty and steel couch* of war   *beds

39

My thrice-driven* bed of down. I do agnize*   *sifted / acknowledge*
A natural and prompt alacrity
I find in hardness,* and do undertake   *hardship*
250 This present wars against the Ottomites.
Most humbly, therefore, bending to your state,*   *power*
I crave fit disposition for my wife,
Due reference of place and exhibition,
With such accommodation and besort*   *suitable attendance*
255 As levels* with her breeding.   *corresponds*

DUKE   Why, at her father's.

BRABANTIO   I will not have it so.

OTHELLO   Nor I.

DESDEMONA   Nor would I there reside
260 To put my father in impatient thoughts
By being in his eye. Most gracious duke,
To my unfolding* lend your prosperous* ear   *explanation / receptive*
And let me find a charter* in your voice   *willingness; immunity*
T' assist my simpleness.

265 DUKE   What would you, Desdemona?

DESDEMONA   That I love the Moor to live with him
My downright violence and storm of fortunes
May trumpet to the world. My heart's subdued
Even to the very quality of my lord.
270 I saw Othello's visage in his mind,
And to his honors and his valiant parts*   *qualities*
Did I my soul and fortunes consecrate.
So that, dear lords, if I be left behind,
A moth of peace, and he go to the war,
275 The rites for why I love him are bereft me
And I a heavy interim shall support*   *bear*
By his dear absence. Let me go with him.

OTHELLO   Let her have your voice.*   *agreement*
Vouch with me, heaven, I therefore beg it not
280 To please the palate of my appetite,
Nor to comply with heat* (the young affects   *desire*
In me defunct) and proper satisfaction,
But to be free and bounteous to her mind.
And heaven defend your good souls that you think
285 I will your serious and great business scant*   *neglect*
For she is with me. No, when light-winged toys*   *pleasures*
Of feathered Cupid seel* with wanton dullness   *close up*
My speculative and officed instruments,*   *faculties*
That* my disports* corrupt and taint my business,   *So that / delight*
290 Let housewives make a skillet of my helm,*   *helmet*
And all indign* and base adversities   *disgraceful*
Make head against my estimation.*   *(attack my reputation)*

DUKE   Be it as you shall privately determine,
Either for her stay or going. Th' affair cries haste,
295 And speed must answer it.

FIRST SENATOR   You must away tonight.

OTHELLO   With all my heart.

DUKE   At nine i' th' morning here we'll meet again.
Othello, leave some officer behind
300 And he shall our commission bring to you,
With such things else of quality and respect*   *importance*
As doth import* you.   *concern*

OTHELLO   So please your Grace, my ancient.
A man he is of honesty and trust.
305 To his conveyance I assign my wife,
With what else needful your good Grace shall think
To be sent after me.

DUKE   Let it be so.
Good night to everyone. [*To Brabantio*] And, noble signior,

310   If virtue no delighted beauty lack,
      Your son-in-law is far more fair than black.

FIRST SENATOR   Adieu, brave Moor, use Desdemona well.

BRABANTIO   Look to* her, Moor, if thou hast eyes to see.   *Watch*
      She has deceived her father, and may thee.   [*He exits.*]

315   OTHELLO   My life upon her faith!
      [*The Duke, the Senators, Cassio, and Officers exit.*]
                                        Honest Iago,
      My Desdemona must I leave to thee.
      I prithee let thy wife attend on her,
      And bring them after in the best advantage.—
320   Come, Desdemona, I have but an hour
      Of love, of worldly matters, and direction
      To spend with thee. We must obey the time.

      [*Othello and Desdemona exit.*]

      RODERIGO   Iago—

      IAGO   What sayst thou, noble heart?

325   RODERIGO   What will I do, think'st thou?

      IAGO   Why, go to bed and sleep.

      RODERIGO   I will incontinently* drown myself.   *immediately*

      IAGO   If thou dost, I shall never love thee after. Why,
      thou silly gentleman!

330   RODERIGO   It is silliness to live, when to live is torment, and then
      have we a prescription to die when death is our physician.

      IAGO   O, villainous! I have looked upon the world for four times
      seven years, and since I could distinguish betwixt a benefit and

43

an injury, I never found man that knew how to love himself. Ere

335 I would say I would drown myself for the love of a guinea hen,*   *prostitute*
I would change my humanity with a baboon.

RODERIGO   What should I do? I confess it is my shame to be so fond,
but it is not in my virtue* to amend it.   *ability*

IAGO   Virtue? A fig!* 'Tis in ourselves that we are thus or thus. Our   *(obscenity)*
340 bodies are our gardens, to the which our wills are gardeners. So that
if we will plant nettles or sow lettuce, set hyssop* and weed up thyme,   *mint*
supply it with one gender* of herbs or distract it with many, either to   *type*
have it sterile with idleness or manured with industry, why the power
and corrigible authority of this lies in our wills. If the balance of
345 our lives had not one scale of reason to poise* another of sensuality,   *counterbalance*
the blood and baseness of our natures would conduct us to most
prepost'rous conclusions. But we have reason to cool our raging motions,*   *impulses*
our carnal stings, our unbitted* lusts—whereof I take this that you   *uncontrolled*
call love to be a sect, or scion.*   *offshoot*

350 RODERIGO   It cannot be.

IAGO   It is merely a lust of the blood and a permission of the will.
Come, be a man! Drown thyself? Drown cats and blind puppies.
I have professed me thy friend, and I confess me knit to thy deserving
with cables of perdurable toughness. I could never better stead*   *help*
355 thee than now. Put money in thy purse. Follow thou the wars; defeat
thy favor* with an usurped beard. I say, put money in thy purse.   *disguise yourself*
It cannot be that Desdemona should long continue her love to the
Moor—put money in thy purse—nor he his to her. It was a violent
commencement* in her, and thou shalt see an answerable   *abrupt affair*
360 sequestration*—put but money in thy purse. These Moors are   *abrupt separation*
changeable in their wills. Fill thy purse with money. The food that
to him now is as luscious as locusts shall be to him shortly as bitter
as coloquintida. She must change for youth.* When she is sated with   *a younger man*
his body she will find the error of her choice. Therefore, put money
365 in thy purse. If thou wilt needs damn thyself, do it a more delicate way
than drowning. Make all the money thou canst. If sanctimony and
a frail vow betwixt an erring barbarian and a supersubtle* Venetian   *deceptive*

be not too hard for my wits and all the tribe of hell, thou shalt enjoy
her. Therefore make money. A pox of drowning thyself! It is clean out
370 of the way. Seek thou rather to be hanged in compassing* thy joy   *achieving
than to be drowned and go without her.

RODERIGO   Wilt thou be fast* to my hopes if I depend on the issue?   *steadfast

IAGO   Thou art sure of me. Go, make money. I have told thee often,
and I retell thee again and again, I hate the Moor. My cause is
375 hearted;* thine hath no less reason. Let us be conjunctive* in   *in my heart | united
our revenge against him. If thou canst cuckold him, thou dost thyself
a pleasure, me a sport. There are many events in the womb of time
which will be delivered. Traverse, go, provide thy money. We will
have more of this tomorrow. Adieu.

380 RODERIGO   Where shall we meet i' th' morning?

IAGO   At my lodging.

RODERIGO   I'll be with thee betimes.*   *early

IAGO   Go to, farewell. Do you hear, Roderigo?

RODERIGO   What say you?

385 IAGO   No more of drowning, do you hear?

RODERIGO   I am changed.

IAGO   Go to, farewell. Put money enough in your purse.

RODERIGO   I'll sell all my land.   [*He exits.*]

IAGO   Thus do I ever make my fool my purse.
390 For I mine own gained knowledge should profane
If I would time expend with such a snipe*   *fools
But for my sport and profit. I hate the Moor,
And it is thought abroad that 'twixt my sheets

’Has done my office. I know not if ’t be true,
395 But I, for mere suspicion in that kind,*   *regard*
Will do* as if for surety.* He holds* me well.   *act | it were true | regards*
The better shall my purpose work on him.
Cassio’s a proper* man. Let me see now: *attractive*
To get his place* and to plume up* my will   *position | enhance*
400 In double knavery—How? how?—Let’s see.
After some time, to abuse Othello’s ear
That he is too familiar with his wife.
He hath a person and a smooth dispose*   *manner*
To be suspected, framed to make women false.
405 The Moor is of a free* and open nature   *sincere*
That thinks men honest that but seem to be so,
And will as tenderly* be led by th’ nose   *easily*
As asses are.
I have ’t. It is engendered. Hell and night
410 Must bring this monstrous birth to the world’s light.

[*He exits.*]

Act 2.

Scene 1.
A seaport in Cyprus

[Enter Montano and two Gentlemen.]

MONTANO   What from the cape can you discern at sea?

FIRST GENTLEMAN   Nothing at all. It is a high-wrought flood.*   *rough sea*
I cannot 'twixt the heaven and the main*   *sea*
Descry a sail.

5   MONTANO   Methinks the wind hath spoke aloud at land.
A fuller blast ne'er shook our battlements.
If it hath ruffianed so upon the sea,
What ribs of oak,* when mountains* melt on them,   *(ship's frame) / mountainous waves*
Can hold the mortise? What shall we hear of this?

10   SECOND GENTLEMAN   A segregation* of the Turkish fleet.   *scattering*
For do but stand upon the foaming shore,
The chidden billow* seems to pelt the clouds,   *sea rebuked by the wind*
The wind-shaked surge, with high and monstrous mane,
Seems to cast water on the burning Bear*   *(Ursa Minor)*
15   And quench the guards of th' ever-fixèd pole.
I never did like molestation view*   *see such disturbance*
On the enchafèd* flood.   *tumultuous*

MONTANO   If that the Turkish fleet
Be not ensheltered and embayed, they are drowned.
20   It is impossible to bear it out.

[Enter a third Gentleman.]

THIRD GENTLEMAN   News, lads! Our wars are done.
The desperate tempest hath so banged the Turks

That their designment* halts. A noble ship of Venice

plan

Hath seen a grievous wrack and sufferance

25   On most part of their fleet.

MONTANO   How? Is this true?

THIRD GENTLEMAN   The ship is here put in,

A Veronesa. Michael Cassio,

Lieutenant to the warlike Moor Othello,

30   Is come on shore; the Moor himself at sea,

And is in full commission here for Cyprus.

MONTANO   I am glad on 't. 'Tis a worthy governor.

THIRD GENTLEMAN   But this same Cassio, though he speak of comfort

Touching* the Turkish loss, yet he looks sadly

About

35   And prays the Moor be safe, for they were parted

With foul and violent tempest.

MONTANO   Pray heaven he be;

For I have served him, and the man commands

Like a full* soldier. Let's to the seaside, ho!

true

40   As well to see the vessel that's come in

As to throw out our eyes for brave Othello,

Even till we make the main* and th' aerial blue*

sea / sky

An indistinct regard.

THIRD GENTLEMAN   Come, let's do so;

45   For every minute is expectancy

Of more arrivance.

[*Enter Cassio.*]

CASSIO   Thanks, you the valiant of this warlike isle,

That so approve the Moor! O, let the heavens

Give him defense against the elements,

50   For I have lost him on a dangerous sea.

MONTANO   Is he well shipped?

CASSIO   His bark* is stoutly timbered, and his pilot   *ship
Of very expert and approved allowance;*   *ability
Therefore my hopes, not surfeited* to death,   *sick from excess
55   Stand in bold cure.

[*Voices cry within. "A sail, a sail, a sail!"*
Enter a Messenger.]

CASSIO   What noise?

MESSENGER   The town is empty; on the brow* o' th' sea   *edge
Stand ranks of people, and they cry "A sail!"

CASSIO   My hopes do shape him for* the Governor.   *make him out to be

[*A shot is heard.*]

60   SECOND GENTLEMAN   They do discharge their shot of courtesy.
Our friends, at least.

CASSIO   I pray you, sir, go forth,
And give us truth who 'tis that is arrived.

SECOND GENTLEMAN   I shall.   [*He exits.*]

65   MONTANO   But, good lieutenant, is your general wived?

CASSIO   Most fortunately. He hath achieved* a maid   *won
That paragons* description and wild fame,*   *surpasses / rumors
One that excels the quirks of blazoning* pens,   *praise-giving
And in th' essential vesture of creation
70   Does tire the ingener.*   *artist
[*Enter second Gentleman.*]
                  How now? Who has put in?

SECOND GENTLEMAN   'Tis one Iago, ancient to the General.

CASSIO 'Has had most favorable and happy speed!
Tempests themselves, high seas, and howling winds,
75 The guttered* rocks and congregated sands   *jagged*
(Traitors ensteeped* to clog the guiltless keel),   *submerged*
As having sense of beauty, do omit*   *forgo*
Their mortal* natures, letting go safely by   *deadly*
The divine Desdemona.

80 MONTANO What is she?

CASSIO She that I spake of, our great captain's captain,
Left in the conduct of the bold Iago,
Whose footing* here anticipates our thoughts   *landing*
A sennight's* speed. Great Jove, Othello guard,*   *week's | guard Othello*
85 And swell his sail with thine own powerful breath,
That he may bless this bay with his tall ship,
Make love's quick pants in Desdemona's arms,
Give renewed fire to our extinct spirits,
And bring all Cyprus comfort!
[*Enter Desdemona, Iago, Roderigo, and Emilia.*]
90   O, behold,
The riches of the ship is come on shore!
You men of Cyprus, let her have your knees.   [*He kneels.*]
Hail to thee, lady, and the grace of heaven,
Before, behind thee, and on every hand
95 Enwheel thee round.   [*He rises.*]

DESDEMONA I thank you, valiant Cassio.
What tidings can you tell of my lord?

CASSIO He is not yet arrived, nor know I aught
But that he's well and will be shortly here.

100 DESDEMONA O, but I fear—How lost you company?

CASSIO The great contention of sea and skies second
Parted our fellowship.

[*Voices cry within "A sail, a sail!" A shot is heard.*]
                    But hark, a sail!

SECOND GENTLEMAN   They give their greeting to the citadel.
105 This likewise is a friend.

CASSIO   See for the news.
[*Second Gentleman exits.*]
Good ancient, you are welcome. Welcome, mistress.
[*He kisses Emilia.*]
Let it not gall your patience, good Iago,
That I extend my manners. 'Tis my breeding
110 That gives me this bold show of courtesy.

IAGO   Sir, would she give you so much of her lips
As of her tongue she oft bestows on me,
You would have enough.

DESDEMONA   Alas, she has no speech!*   *says nothing*

115 IAGO   In faith, too much.
I find it still when I have list to sleep.
Marry, before your Ladyship, I grant,
She puts her tongue a little in her heart
And chides with thinking.

120 EMILIA   You have little cause to say so.

IAGO   Come on, come on! You* are pictures* out of door,   *Women / silent*
bells* in your parlors, wildcats* in your kitchens, saints in your   *noisy / territorial*
injuries, devils being offended, players* in your housewifery,   *deceptive*
and housewives in your beds.

125 DESDEMONA   Oh, fie upon thee, slanderer.

IAGO   Nay, it is true, or else I am a Turk.
You rise to play, and go to bed to work.

EMILIA   You shall not write my praise.

IAGO   No, let me not.

130 DESDEMONA   What wouldst write of me if thou shouldst praise me?

IAGO   O, gentle lady, do not put me to 't,
For I am nothing if not critical.

DESDEMONA   Come on, assay.*—There's one gone to the harbor?   *try*

IAGO   Ay, madam.

135 DESDEMONA   [*aside*] I am not merry, but I do beguile*   *disguise*
The thing I am* by seeming otherwise.—   *(my worries)*
Come, how wouldst thou praise me?

IAGO   I am about it, but indeed my invention comes from my pate*   *head*
as birdlime does from frieze: it plucks out brains and all. But my muse
140 labors,* and thus she is delivered: *gives birth*
"If she be fair* and wise, fairness and wit,   *fair-skinned*
The one's for use, the other useth it."

DESDEMONA   Well praised! How if she be black and witty?

IAGO   "If she be black,* and thereto have a wit,   *dark-skinned*
145 She'll find a white* that shall her blackness fit."   *person*

DESDEMONA   Worse and worse.

EMILIA   How if fair and foolish?

IAGO   "She never yet was foolish that was fair,
For even her folly* helped her to an heir."   *foolishness*

150 DESDEMONA   These are old fond* paradoxes to make fools laugh   *foolish*
i' th' alehouse. What miserable praise hast thou for her that's foul*   *ugly*
and foolish?

IAGO   "There's none so foul and foolish thereunto,*   *besides*
But does foul* pranks which fair and wise ones do."   *vile*

155 DESDEMONA   O heavy ignorance! Thou praisest the worst best.
But what praise couldst thou bestow on a deserving woman indeed,
one that in the authority of her merit did justly put on the vouch*   *demand the approval*
of very malice itself?

IAGO   "She that was ever fair and never proud,
160 Had tongue at will and yet was never loud,
Never lacked gold and yet went never gay,*   *well dressed*
Fled from her wish, and yet said "Now I may,"*   *withstood temptation*
She that being angered, her revenge being nigh,
Bade her wrong stay* and her displeasure fly,   *endured injury patiently*
165 She that in wisdom never was so frail
To change the cod's head for the salmon's tail,*   *(unworthy exchange; sexual)*
She that could think and ne'er disclose her mind,
See suitors following and not look behind,
She was a wight,* if ever such wights were"—   *person*

170 DESDEMONA   To do what?

IAGO   "To suckle* fools and chronicle small beer."*   *breastfeed | domestic goods*

DESDEMONA   O, most lame and impotent conclusion!—Do not
learn of him, Emilia, though he be thy husband.—How say you,
Cassio? Is he not a most profane and liberal* counselor?   *unrestrained*

175 CASSIO   He speaks home,* madam. You may relish him more in*   *bluntly | as*
the soldier than in the scholar.   [*Cassio takes Desdemona's hand.*]

IAGO   [*aside*] He takes her by the palm. Ay, well said, whisper. With
as little a web as this will I ensnare as great a fly as Cassio. Ay, smile
upon her, do. I will gyve* thee in thine own courtship.* You say true,   *shackle | courtliness*
180 'tis so indeed. If such tricks as these strip you out of your lieutenantry,
it had been better you had not kissed your three fingers so oft, which
now again you are most apt to play the sir* in. Very good; well kissed;   *gentleman*
an excellent courtesy! 'Tis so, indeed. Yet again your fingers to your lips?

Would they were clyster-pipes* for your sake!   *enema tubes
[*Trumpets within.*]
185 The Moor. I know his trumpet.

CASSIO   'Tis truly so.

DESDEMONA   Let's meet him and receive him.

CASSIO   Lo, where he comes!

[*Enter Othello and Attendants.*]

OTHELLO   O, my fair warrior!

190 DESDEMONA   My dear Othello!

OTHELLO   It gives me wonder great as my content
To see you here before me. O my soul's joy!
If after every tempest come such calms,
May the winds blow till they have wakened death,
195 And let the laboring bark* climb hills of seas   *ship
Olympus high, and duck again as low
As hell's from heaven! If it were now to die,
'Twere now to be most happy, for I fear
My soul hath her content so absolute
200 That not another comfort like to this
Succeeds* in unknown fate.*   *follows / future

DESDEMONA   The heavens forbid
But that our loves and comforts should increase
Even as our days do grow!

205 OTHELLO   Amen to that, sweet powers!
I cannot speak enough of this content.
It stops me here; it is too much of joy.
[*Desdemona and Othello kiss.*]
And this, and this, the greatest discords be
That e'er our hearts shall make!

IAGO   [*aside*] O, you are well tuned now,
210 But I'll set down the pegs that make this music,
As honest as I am.

OTHELLO   Come. Let us to the castle.—
News, friends! Our wars are done. The Turks are drowned.
215 How does my old acquaintance of this isle?—
Honey, you shall be well desired* in Cyprus.   *loved*
I have found great love amongst them. O, my sweet,
I prattle out of fashion,* and I dote   *inappropriately*
In mine own comforts.—I prithee, good Iago,
220 Go to the bay and disembark my coffers.
Bring thou the master* to the citadel.   *captain*
He is a good one, and his worthiness
Does challenge* much respect.—Come, Desdemona.   *deserve*
Once more, well met at Cyprus.

[*All but Iago and Roderigo exit.*]

225 IAGO   [*to a departing Attendant*] Do thou meet me presently at the
harbor. [*To Roderigo*] Come hither. If thou be'st valiant—as they say
base* men being in love have then a nobility in their natures more   *lowly born*
than is native to them—list* me. The Lieutenant tonight watches on   *listen to*
the court of guard. First, I must tell thee this: Desdemona is directly
230 in love with him.

RODERIGO   With him? Why, 'tis not possible.

IAGO   [*putting a finger to his lips*] Lay thy finger thus, and let thy soul
be instructed. Mark me with what violence she first loved the Moor
but for bragging and telling her fantastical lies. And will she love him
235 still for prating? Let not thy discreet heart think it. Her eye must be
fed. And what delight shall she have to look on the devil? When the
blood* is made dull with the act of sport,* there should be, again   *appetite* / *lovemaking*
to inflame it and to give satiety a fresh appetite, loveliness in favor,*   *look*
sympathy* in years, manners, and beauties, all which the Moor   *agreement*
240 is defective in. Now, for want of these required conveniences,*   *agreements*
her delicate tenderness will find itself abused,* begin to heave the   *mistreated*

gorge,* disrelish and abhor the Moor. Very nature will instruct her *feel nausea*
in it and compel her to some second choice. Now, sir, this granted—
as it is a most pregnant* and unforced position—who stands so *obvious*
245 eminent in the degree of this fortune as Cassio does? A knave* *villain*
very voluble,* no further conscionable* than in putting on the mere *glib / ethical*
form of civil and humane* seeming for the better compassing* *courteous / attaining*
of his salt* and most hidden loose affection. Why, none, why, none! *lewd*
A slipper* and subtle knave, a finder of occasions, that has an eye can *slippery*
250 stamp and counterfeit advantages, though true advantage never present
itself; a devilish knave! Besides, the knave is handsome, young, and
hath all those requisites in him that folly* and green minds look after. *wantonness*
A pestilent complete knave, and the woman hath found him already.

RODERIGO   I cannot believe that in her. She's full of most
255 blessed condition.

IAGO   Blessed fig's end!* The wine she drinks is made of grapes. *(obscenity)*
If she had been blessed, she would never have loved the Moor.
Blessed pudding!* Didst thou not see her paddle with the palm of *sausage*
his hand? Didst not mark that?

260 RODERIGO   Yes, that I did. But that was but courtesy.

IAGO   Lechery, by this hand! An index and obscure prologue to
the history of lust and foul thoughts. They met so near with their
lips that their breaths embraced together. Villainous thoughts,
Roderigo! When these mutualities* so marshal the way, hard *exchange of intimacies*
265 at hand* comes the master and main exercise, th' incorporate* *immediately / physical*
conclusion. Pish! But, sir, be you ruled by me. I have brought you
from Venice. Watch you tonight.* For the command, I'll lay 't upon *Stand watch*
you. Cassio knows you not. I'll not be far from you. Do you find
some occasion to anger Cassio, either by speaking too loud, or
270 tainting* his discipline, or from what other course you please, *insulting*
which the time shall more favorably minister.* *provide*

RODERIGO   Well.

IAGO   Sir, he's rash and very sudden in choler,* and haply* may strike   *anger / perhaps*
at you. Provoke him that he may, for even out of that will I cause these
275 of Cyprus to mutiny, whose qualification shall come into no true taste
again but by the displanting of Cassio. So shall you have a shorter
journey to your desires by the means I shall then have to prefer* them,   *promote*
and the impediment most profitably removed, without the which
there were no expectation of our prosperity.

280 RODERIGO   I will do this, if you can bring it to any opportunity.

IAGO   I warrant thee. Meet me by and by at the citadel. I must
fetch his necessaries* ashore. Farewell.   *Othello's belongings*

RODERIGO   Adieu.   [*He exits.*]

IAGO   That Cassio loves her, I do well believe 't.
285 That she loves him, 'tis apt and of great credit.*   *likely and believable*
The Moor, howbeit that I endure him not,
Is of a constant, loving, noble nature,
And I dare think he'll prove to Desdemona
A most dear husband. Now, I do love her too,
290 Not out of absolute lust (though peradventure*   *perhaps*
I stand accountant* for as great a sin)   *accountable*
But partly led to diet* my revenge   *feed*
For that I do suspect the lusty Moor
Hath leaped into my seat*—the thought whereof   *slept with my wife*
295 Doth, like a poisonous mineral, gnaw my inwards,*   *innards*
And nothing can or shall content my soul
Till I am evened with him, wife for wife,
Or, failing so, yet that I put the Moor
At least into a jealousy so strong
300 That judgment cannot cure. Which thing to do,
If this poor trash of Venice, whom I trace
For his quick hunting, stand the putting on,
I'll have our Michael Cassio on the hip,*   *at a disadvantage*
Abuse* him to the Moor in the rank garb*   *slander / manner*
305 (For I fear Cassio with my nightcap* too),   *wife*
Make the Moor thank me, love me, and reward me

For making him egregiously an ass
And practicing upon* his peace and quiet   *destroying
Even to madness. 'Tis here,* but yet confused.   *My plan is here
310 Knavery's plain face is never seen till used.

[*He exits.*]

Scene 2.
A street in Cyprus

[*Enter Othello's Herald with a proclamation.*]

HERALD   It is Othello's pleasure, our noble and valiant general, that
upon certain tidings now arrived, importing the mere perdition* of   *destruction*
the Turkish fleet, every man put himself into triumph: some to dance,
some to make bonfires, each man to what sport and revels his addition*   *rank*
5   leads him. For besides these beneficial news, it is the celebration of
his nuptial. So much was his pleasure should be proclaimed. All offices*   *kitchens*
are open, and there is full liberty of feasting from this present hour of
five till the bell have told eleven. Heaven bless the isle of Cyprus and
our noble general, Othello!

[*He exits.*]

Scene 3.
The citadel at Cyprus

[*Enter Othello, Desdemona, Cassio, and Attendants.*]

OTHELLO   Good Michael, look you to the guard tonight.
Let's teach ourselves that honorable stop*   *restraint*
Not to outsport* discretion.   *pass the limits of*

CASSIO   Iago hath direction what to do,
5   But notwithstanding, with my personal eye
Will I look to 't.

OTHELLO   Iago is most honest.
Michael, goodnight. Tomorrow with your earliest
Let me have speech with you. [*To Desdemona*] Come, my dear love,
10   The purchase* made, the fruits* are to ensue;   *marriage | consumation*
That profit's yet to come 'tween me and you.—
Goodnight.

[*Othello and Desdemona exit, with Attendants.
Enter Iago.*]

CASSIO   Welcome, Iago. We must to the watch.

IAGO   Not this hour, lieutenant. 'Tis not yet ten o' th' clock.
15   Our general cast* us thus early for the love of his Desdemona—   *dismissed*
who let us not therefore blame; he hath not yet made wanton
the night with her, and she is sport for Jove.

CASSIO   She's a most exquisite lady.

IAGO   And, I'll warrant her, full of game.*   *spirit; (sexual)*

20   CASSIO   Indeed, she's a most fresh and delicate creature.

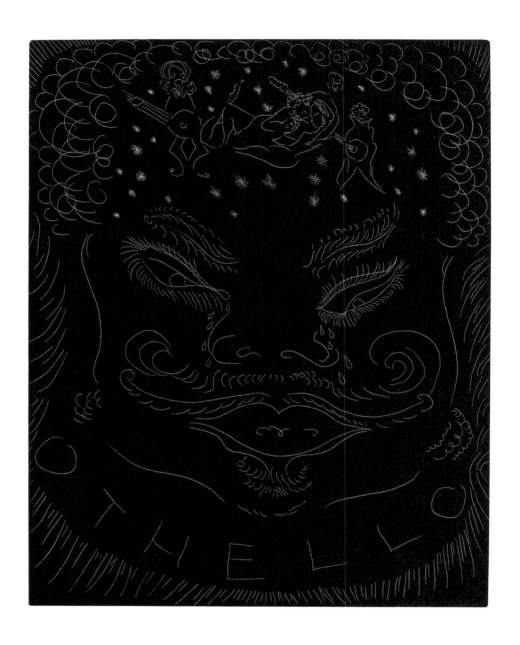

Consummation

IAGO   What an eye she has! Methinks it sounds a parley*   *military call
to provocation.

CASSIO   An inviting eye, and yet methinks right* modest.   *very

IAGO   And when she speaks, is it not an alarum* to love?   *call to arms

25   CASSIO   She is indeed perfection.

IAGO   Well, happiness to their sheets! Come, lieutenant, I have a stoup*   *bottle
of wine; and here without* are a brace of* Cyprus gallants   *outside | pair
that would fain have a measure* to the health of black Othello.   *like to drink

CASSIO   Not tonight, good Iago. I have very poor and unhappy
30   brains for drinking. I could well wish courtesy would invent some
other custom of entertainment.

IAGO   O, they are our friends! But one cup; I'll drink for you.

CASSIO   I have drunk but one cup tonight, and that was craftily
qualified* too, and behold what innovation* it makes here. I am   *diluted | change
35   unfortunate in the infirmity and dare not task my weakness with
any more.

IAGO   What, man! 'Tis a night of revels. The gallants desire it.

CASSIO   Where are they?

IAGO   Here at the door. I pray you, call them in.

40   CASSIO   I'll do 't, but it dislikes* me.   [He exits.]   *displeases

IAGO   If I can fasten but one cup upon him
With that which he hath drunk tonight already,
He'll be as full of quarrel and offense
As my young mistress' dog. Now my sick fool Roderigo,
45   Whom love hath turned almost the wrong side out,
To Desdemona hath tonight caroused

Potations pottle-deep;* and he's to watch.   *drunk two quartfuls*
Three else of Cyprus, noble swelling spirits
That hold their honors in a wary distance,
50   The very elements* of this warlike isle,   *characteristics*
Have I tonight flustered with flowing cups;
And they watch too. Now, 'mongst this flock of drunkards
Am I to put our Cassio in some action*   *fight*
That may offend the isle. But here they come.
55   If consequence do but approve my dream,*   *events go my way*
My boat sails freely both with wind and stream.

[*Enter Cassio, Montano, and Gentlemen, followed by Servants with wine.*]

CASSIO   'Fore God, they have given me a rouse* already.   *full drink*

MONTANO   Good faith, a little one; not past a pint, as I am a soldier.

IAGO   Some wine, ho!
60   [*Sings.*] *And let me the cannikin* clink, clink,*   *drinking vessel*
And let me the cannikin clink.
A soldier's a man,
O, man's life's but a span,
Why, then, let a soldier drink.
65   Some wine, boys!

CASSIO   'Fore God, an excellent song.

IAGO   I learned it in England, where indeed they are most potent
in potting.* Your Dane, your German, and your swag-bellied Hollander   *drinking*
—drink, ho!—are nothing to your English.

70   CASSIO   Is your Englishman so exquisite in his drinking?

IAGO   Why, he drinks you, with facility, your Dane dead drunk.
He sweats not to overthrow your Almain.* He gives your Hollander   *German*
a vomit ere the next pottle* can be filled.   *tankard*

CASSIO   To the health of our general!

MONTANO   I am for it, lieutenant, and I'll do you justice.

IAGO   O sweet England!
[*Sings.*] *King Stephen was and a worthy peer,*
His breeches cost him but a crown;
He held them sixpence all too dear;
80 *With that he called the tailor lown.**   rogue
He was a wight of high renown,*   person
And thou art but of low degree;
'Tis pride that pulls the country down,
Then take thy auld cloak about thee.
85 Some wine, ho!

CASSIO   'Fore God, this is a more exquisite song than the other!

IAGO   Will you hear 't again?

CASSIO   No, for I hold him to be unworthy of his place* that does   rank
those things. Well, God's above all; and there be souls must be saved,
90 and there be souls must not be saved.

IAGO   It's true, good lieutenant.

CASSIO   For mine own part—no offense to the General,
nor any man of quality*—I hope to be saved.   rank

IAGO   And so do I too, lieutenant.

95 CASSIO   Ay, but, by your leave, not before me. The Lieutenant is to be
saved before the Ancient. Let's have no more of this. Let's to our affairs.
God forgive us our sins! Gentlemen, let's look to our business. Do not
think, gentlemen, I am drunk. This is my ancient, this is my right hand,
and this is my left. I am not drunk now. I can stand well enough, and
100 I speak well enough.

GENTLEMEN   Excellent well.

CASSIO   Why, very well then. You must not think then that I am drunk.
[*He exits.*]

MONTANO   To th' platform,* masters. Come, let's set the watch.   *gun

[*Gentlemen exit.*]

IAGO   [*to Montano*] You see this fellow that is gone before?
105 He's a soldier fit to stand by Caesar
And give direction; and do but see his vice.
'Tis to his virtue a just equinox,*   *equivalent size
The one as long as th' other. 'Tis pity of him.*   *It's a shame
I fear the trust Othello puts him in,
110 On some odd time of his infirmity,
Will shake this island.

MONTANO   But is he often thus?

IAGO   'Tis evermore the prologue to his sleep.
He'll watch the horologe* a double set*   *clock / night and day
115 If drink rock not his cradle.

MONTANO   It were well
The General were put in mind of it.
Perhaps he sees it not, or his good nature
Prizes the virtue that appears in Cassio
120 And looks not on his evils. Is not this true?

[*Enter Roderigo.*]

IAGO   [*aside to Roderigo*] How now, Roderigo?
I pray you, after the Lieutenant, go.

[*Roderigo exits.*]

MONTANO   And 'tis great pity that the noble Moor
Should hazard such a place as his own second
125 With one of an engraffed* infirmity.   *ingrained
It were an honest action to say so
To the Moor.

IAGO   Not I, for this fair island.
I do love Cassio well and would do much
130 To cure him of this evil— ["Help, help!" within.] But hark! What noise?

[Enter Cassio, pursuing Roderigo.]

CASSIO   Zounds, you rogue, you rascal!

MONTANO   What's the matter, lieutenant?

CASSIO   A knave teach me my duty? I'll beat the knave into
a twiggen* bottle.   *wicker-cased*

135 RODERIGO   Beat me?

CASSIO   Dost thou prate, rogue?   [He hits Roderigo.]

MONTANO   Nay, good lieutenant. I pray you, sir, hold your hand.

CASSIO   Let me go, sir, or I'll knock you o'er the mazard.*   *head*

MONTANO   Come, come, you're drunk.

140 CASSIO   Drunk?

[They fight.]

IAGO   [aside to Roderigo] Away, I say! Go out and cry a mutiny.
[Roderigo exits.]
Nay, good lieutenant.—God's will, gentlemen!—
Help, ho! Lieutenant—sir—Montano—sir—
Help, masters!—Here's a goodly watch indeed!
[A bell is rung.]
145 Who's that which rings the bell? Diablo,* ho!   *Devil*
The town will rise. God's will, lieutenant, hold!
You will be shamed forever.

[Enter Othello and Attendants.]

OTHELLO   What is the matter here?

MONTANO   Zounds, I bleed still. I am hurt to th' death. He dies!
[*He attacks Cassio.*]

150 OTHELLO   Hold, for your lives!

IAGO   Hold, ho! Lieutenant—sir—Montano—gentlemen—
Have you forgot all sense of place and duty?
Hold! The General speaks to you. Hold, for shame!

OTHELLO   Why, how now, ho! From whence ariseth this?
155 Are we turned Turks, and to ourselves do that
Which heaven hath forbid the Ottomites?
For Christian shame, put by this barbarous brawl!
He that stirs next to carve for his own rage*   *draw a sword in anger*
Holds his soul light; he dies upon his motion.
160 Silence that dreadful bell. It frights the isle
From her propriety. What is the matter, masters?
Honest Iago, that looks dead with grieving,
Speak. Who began this? On thy love, I charge thee.

IAGO   I do not know. Friends all but now, even now,
165 In quarter* and in terms like bride and groom   *Under control*
Divesting them* for bed; and then but now,   *Getting undressed*
As if some planet had unwitted men,
Swords out, and tilting one at other's breast,
In opposition bloody. I cannot speak
170 Any beginning to this peevish odds,*   *strife*
And would in action glorious I had lost
Those legs that brought me to a part of it!

OTHELLO   How comes it, Michael, you are thus forgot?*   *forgot yourself*

CASSIO   I pray you pardon me; I cannot speak.

175 OTHELLO   Worthy Montano, you were wont be* civil.   *used to be*
The gravity and stillness of your youth

The world hath noted. And your name is great
In mouths of wisest censure.* What's the matter   *judgment*
That you unlace your reputation thus,
180 And spend* your rich opinion* for the name   *squander / reputation*
Of a night-brawler? Give me answer to it.

MONTANO   Worthy Othello, I am hurt to danger.
Your officer Iago can inform you,
While I spare speech, which something now offends me,*   *pains me*
185 Of all that I do know; nor know I aught*   *anything*
By me that's said or done amiss this night,
Unless self-charity be sometimes a vice,
And to defend ourselves it be a sin
When violence assails us.

190 OTHELLO   Now, by heaven,
My blood begins my safer guides to rule,
And passion, having my best judgment collied,*   *darkened*
Assays* to lead the way. Zounds, if I stir,   *Tries*
Or do but lift this arm, the best of you
195 Shall sink in my rebuke. Give me to know
How this foul rout began, who set it on;
And he that is approved in* this offense,   *proved guilty of*
Though he had twinned with me, both at a birth,
Shall lose me.* What, in a town of war   *my favor*
200 Yet wild, the people's hearts brimful of fear,
To manage* private and domestic quarrel,   *carry on*
In night, and on the court and guard of safety?
'Tis monstrous. Iago, who began 't?

MONTANO   If partially affined, or leagued* in office,   *bias (in favor of Cassio)*
205 Thou dost deliver more or less than truth,
Thou art no soldier.

IAGO   Touch me not so near.
I had rather have this tongue cut from my mouth
Than it should do offense to Michael Cassio.
210 Yet I persuade myself, to speak the truth

Shall nothing wrong him. Thus it is, general:
Montano and myself being in speech,
There comes a fellow crying out for help,
And Cassio following him with determined sword
215 To execute upon* him. Sir, this gentleman [*pointing to Montano*]   *attack*
Steps in to Cassio and entreats his pause.
Myself the crying fellow did pursue,
Lest by his clamor—as it so fell out*—   *happened*
The town might fall in fright. He, swift of foot,
220 Outran my purpose, and I returned the rather
For that* I heard the clink and fall of swords   *Because*
And Cassio high in oath, which till tonight
I ne'er might say before. When I came back—
For this was brief—I found them close together
225 At blow and thrust, even as again they were
When you yourself did part them.
More of this matter cannot I report.
But men are men; the best sometimes forget.
Though Cassio did some little wrong to him,
230 As men in rage strike those that wish them best,
Yet surely Cassio, I believe, received
From him that fled some strange indignity
Which patience could not pass.*   *let pass*

OTHELLO   I know, Iago,
235 Thy honesty and love doth mince* this matter,   *minimize*
Making it light to Cassio.—Cassio, I love thee,
But nevermore be officer of mine.
[*Enter Desdemona attended.*]
Look if my gentle love be not raised up!
I'll make thee an example.

240 DESDEMONA   What is the matter, dear?

OTHELLO   All's well now, sweeting.
Come away to bed. [*To Montano*] Sir, for your hurts,
Myself will be your surgeon.—Lead him off.
[*Montano is led off.*]

Iago, look with care about the town
And silence those whom this vile brawl distracted.—
Come, Desdemona. 'Tis the soldier's life
To have their balmy slumbers waked with strife.

245

[*All but Iago and Cassio exit.*]

IAGO   What, are you hurt, lieutenant?

CASSIO   Ay, past all surgery.

250   IAGO   Marry,* God forbid!   *Indeed*

CASSIO   Reputation, reputation, reputation! O, I have lost my
reputation! I have lost the immortal part of myself, and what remains
is bestial. My reputation, Iago, my reputation!

IAGO   As I am an honest man, I thought you had received some bodily
wound. There is more sense in that than in reputation. Reputation is
an idle and most false imposition,* oft got without merit and lost   *artificial notion*
without deserving. You have lost no reputation at all, unless you repute
yourself such a loser. What, man, there are ways to recover the General
again! You are but now cast in his mood—a punishment more in policy
than in malice, even so as one would beat his offenseless dog to affright
an imperious lion. Sue to* him again and he's yours.   *Petition*

255

260

CASSIO   I will rather sue to be despised than to deceive so good
a commander with so slight, so drunken, and so indiscreet an officer.
Drunk? And speak parrot?* And squabble? Swagger? Swear? And   *rant on*
discourse fustian* with one's own shadow? O thou invisible spirit   *nonsense*
of wine, if thou hast no name to be known by, let us call thee devil!

265

IAGO   What was he that you followed with your sword?
What had he done to you?

CASSIO   I know not.

270   IAGO   Is 't possible?

CASSIO   I remember a mass of things, but nothing distinctly; a quarrel,
but nothing wherefore. O God, that men should put an enemy in
their mouths* to steal away their brains! That we should with joy,   *should drink*
pleasance, revel, and applause transform ourselves into beasts!

275   IAGO   Why, but you are now well enough. How came you thus recovered?

CASSIO   It hath pleased the devil drunkenness to give place to
the devil wrath. One unperfectness shows me another, to make me
frankly despise myself.

IAGO   Come, you are too severe a moraler.* As the time, the place,   *moralizer*
280   and the condition of this country stands, I could heartily wish this
had not so befallen. But since it is as it is, mend it for your own good.

CASSIO   I will ask him for my place again; he shall tell me I am
a drunkard! Had I as many mouths as Hydra, such an answer would
stop them all. To be now a sensible man, by and by a fool, and
285   presently a beast! O, strange! Every inordinate cup is unblessed,
and the ingredient is a devil.

IAGO   Come, come, good wine is a good familiar creature, if it be
well used. Exclaim no more against it. And, good lieutenant, I think
you think I love you.

290   CASSIO   I have well approved* it, sir.—I drunk!   *tested*

IAGO   You or any man living may be drunk at a time, man. I'll tell
you what you shall do. Our general's wife is now the general: I may
say so in this respect, for that he hath devoted and given up himself
to the contemplation, mark, and denotement* of her parts*   *description / qualities*
295   and graces. Confess yourself freely to her. Importune her help to put
you in your place* again. She is of so free, so kind, so apt, so blessed   *office*
a disposition she holds it a vice in her goodness not to do more than
she is requested. This broken joint between you and her husband
entreat her to splinter, and, my fortunes against any lay* worth   *wager*
300   naming, this crack of your love shall grow stronger than it was before.

CASSIO   You advise me well.

IAGO   I protest,* in the sincerity of love and honest kindness.   *insist*

CASSIO   I think it freely;* and betimes* in the morning I will beseech   *believe it / early*
the virtuous Desdemona to undertake for me. I am desperate of
305   my fortunes if they check* me here.   *stop*

IAGO   You are in the right. Good night, lieutenant. I must to the watch.

CASSIO   Good night, honest Iago.   [*He exits.*]

IAGO   And what's he, then, that says I play the villain,
When this advice is free I give and honest,
310   Probal* to thinking, and indeed the course   *Wise*
To win the Moor again? For 'tis most easy
Th' inclining* Desdemona to subdue   *The well-disposed*
In any honest suit. She's framed as fruitful*   *generous*
As the free* elements. And then for her   *honorable*
315   To win the Moor—were 't to renounce his baptism,
All seals and symbols of redeemèd sin—
His soul is so enfettered to her love
That she may make, unmake, do what she list,*   *likes*
Even as her appetite* shall play the god   *desire (for Othello)*
320   With his weak function.* How am I then a villain   *(intellectual powers)*
To counsel Cassio to this parallel* course   *suitable*
Directly to his good? Divinity* of hell!   *Theology*
When devils will the blackest sins put on,
They do suggest at first with heavenly shows,
325   As I do now. For whiles this honest fool
Plies Desdemona to repair his fortune,
And she for him pleads strongly to the Moor,
I'll pour this pestilence into his ear:
That she repeals him* for her body's lust;   *appeals for him*
330   And by how much she strives to do him good,
She shall undo her credit with the Moor.
So will I turn her virtue into pitch,

And out of her own goodness make the net
That shall enmesh them all.
[*Enter Roderigo.*]
335   How now, Roderigo?

RODERIGO   I do follow here in the chase, not like a hound that hunts,
but one that fills up the cry. My money is almost spent, I have been
tonight exceedingly well cudgeled, and I think the issue will be I shall
have so much* experience for my pains, and so, with no money at all   *only this*
340   and a little more wit, return again to Venice.

IAGO   How poor are they that have not patience!
What wound did ever heal but by degrees?
Thou know'st we work by wit and not by witchcraft,
And wit depends on dilatory* time.   *drawn out*
345   Does 't not go well? Cassio hath beaten thee,
And thou, by that small hurt, hast cashiered* Cassio.   *dismissed*
Though other things grow fair against the sun,
Yet fruits that blossom first will first be ripe.
Content thyself awhile. By th' Mass, 'tis morning!
350   Pleasure and action make the hours seem short.
Retire thee; go where thou art billeted.
Away, I say! Thou shalt know more hereafter.
Nay, get thee gone.
[*Roderigo exits.*]
                                    Two things are to be done.
355   My wife must move for Cassio to her mistress.
I'll set her on.
Myself the while to draw the Moor apart
And bring him jump* when he may Cassio find   *exactly*
Soliciting his wife. Ay, that's the way.
360   Dull not device by coldness and delay.

[*He exits.*]

Act 3.

Scene 1.
Outside Othello and Desdemona's room

[*Enter Cassio with Musicians.*]

CASSIO Masters, play here (I will content* your pains)
Something that's brief; and bid "Good morrow, general."

reward

[*They play.
Enter the Clown.*]

CLOWN Why masters, have your instruments been in Naples,
that they speak i' th' nose* thus?

(sound nasal)

5 MUSICIAN How, sir, how?

CLOWN Are these, I pray you, wind instruments?

MUSICIAN Ay, marry, are they, sir.

CLOWN O, thereby hangs a tail.

MUSICIAN Whereby hangs a tale, sir?

10 CLOWN Marry, sir, by many a wind instrument that I know. But,
masters, here's money for you; and the General so likes your music
that he desires you, for love's sake, to make no more noise with it.

MUSICIAN Well, sir, we will not.

CLOWN If you have any music that may not be heard, to 't again.
15 But, as they say, to hear music the General does not greatly care.

MUSICIAN   We have none such, sir.

CLOWN   Then put up your pipes in your bag, for I'll away. Go,
vanish into air, away!

[*Musicians exit.*]

CASSIO   Dost thou hear, mine honest friend?

20   CLOWN   No, I hear not your honest friend. I hear you.

CASSIO   Prithee, keep up thy quillets.*   [*Giving money*]   *put away your puns*
There's a poor piece of gold for thee. If the gentlewoman that attends
the General's wife be stirring, tell her there's one Cassio entreats her
a little favor of speech. Wilt thou do this?

25   CLOWN   She is stirring, sir. If she will stir hither, I shall seem*   *arrange*
to notify unto her.

CASSIO   Do, good my friend.   [*Clown exits.*]
[*Enter Iago.*]   In happy time, Iago.

IAGO   You have not been abed, then?

30   CASSIO   Why, no. The day had broke
Before we parted. I have made bold, Iago,
To send in to your wife. My suit* to her   *petition*
Is that she will to virtuous Desdemona
Procure me some access.

35   IAGO   I'll send her to you presently,*   *immediately*
And I'll devise a mean to draw the Moor
Out of the way, that your converse and business
May be more free.

CASSIO   I humbly thank you for 't.
[*Iago exits.*]

I never knew
A Florentine more kind and honest.

[*Enter Emilia.*]

EMILIA   Good morrow, good lieutenant. I am sorry
For your displeasure,* but all will sure be well.   *troubles*
The General and his wife are talking of it,
45   And she speaks for you stoutly. The Moor replies
That he you hurt is of great fame in Cyprus
And great affinity,* and that in wholesome wisdom   *connections*
He might not but refuse you. But he protests he loves you
And needs no other suitor* but his likings   *petitioner*
50   To take the safest occasion by the front
To bring you in again.

CASSIO   Yet I beseech you,
If you think fit, or that it may be done,
Give me advantage of some brief discourse
55   With Desdemon alone.

EMILIA   Pray you come in.
I will bestow you where you shall have time
To speak your bosom* freely.   *inner thoughts; heart*

CASSIO   I am much bound to you.

[*They exit.*]

Scene 2.
The citadel

[*Enter Othello, Iago, and Gentlemen.*]

OTHELLO   These letters give, Iago, to the pilot
And by him do my duties* to the Senate.   *pay my respects*
[*He gives Iago some papers.*]
That done, I will be walking on the works.*   *fortifications*
Repair there to me.

5   IAGO   Well, my good lord, I'll do 't.

OTHELLO   This fortification, gentlemen, shall we see 't?

GENTLEMEN   We wait upon your Lordship.

[*They exit.*]

Scene 3.
The citadel's garden

[*Enter Desdemona, Cassio, and Emilia.*]

DESDEMONA   Be thou assured, good Cassio, I will do
All my abilities in thy behalf.

EMILIA   Good madam, do. I warrant it grieves my husband
As if the cause were his.

5   DESDEMONA   O, that's an honest fellow! Do not doubt, Cassio,
But I will have my lord and you again
As friendly as you were.

CASSIO   Bounteous madam,
Whatever shall become of Michael Cassio,
10   He's never anything but your true servant.

DESDEMONA   I know 't. I thank you. You do love my lord;
You have known him long; and be you well assured
He shall in strangeness* stand no farther off   *distance*
Than in a politic distance.*   *diplomacy requires*

15   CASSIO   Ay, but, lady,
That policy may either last so long,
Or feed upon such nice* and waterish* diet,   *fastidious | thin*
Or breed itself so out of circumstance,
That, I being absent and my place supplied,*   *filled*
20   My general will forget my love and service.

DESDEMONA   Do not doubt* that. Before Emilia here,   *fear*
I give thee warrant* of thy place. Assure thee,   *assurance*
If I do vow a friendship, I'll perform it
To the last article. My lord shall never rest:

25 I'll watch him tame and talk him out of patience;
His bed shall seem a school, his board* a shrift;* *dining table | confessional*
I'll intermingle everything he does
With Cassio's suit. Therefore be merry, Cassio,
For thy solicitor* shall rather die *advocate*
30 Than give thy cause away.

[Enter Othello and Iago.]

EMILIA Madam, here comes my lord.

CASSIO Madam, I'll take my leave.

DESDEMONA Why, stay, and hear me speak.

CASSIO Madam, not now. I am very ill at ease,
35 Unfit for mine own purposes.

DESDEMONA Well, do your discretion.

[Cassio exits.]

IAGO Ha, I like not that.

OTHELLO What dost thou say?

IAGO Nothing, my lord; or if—I know not what.

40 OTHELLO Was not that Cassio parted from my wife?

IAGO Cassio, my lord? No, sure, I cannot think it
That he would steal away so guiltylike,
Seeing your coming.

OTHELLO I do believe 'twas he.

45 DESDEMONA How now, my lord?
I have been talking with a suitor* here, *petitioner*
A man that languishes in your displeasure.

OTHELLO   Who is 't you mean?

DESDEMONA   Why, your lieutenant, Cassio. Good my lord,
50   If I have any grace or power to move you,
His present reconciliation take;*   *accept him*
For if he be not one that truly loves you,
That errs in ignorance and not in cunning,*   *deliberately*
I have no judgment in an honest face.
55   I prithee call him back.

OTHELLO   Went he hence now?

DESDEMONA   Yes, faith, so humbled
That he hath left part of his grief with me
To suffer with him. Good love, call him back.

60   OTHELLO   Not now, sweet Desdemon. Some other time.

DESDEMONA   But shall 't be shortly?

OTHELLO   The sooner, sweet, for you.

DESDEMONA   Shall 't be tonight at supper?

OTHELLO   No, not tonight.

65   DESDEMONA   Tomorrow dinner,* then?   *midday meal*

OTHELLO   I shall not dine at home;
I meet the captains at the citadel.

DESDEMONA   Why then tomorrow night, or Tuesday morn,
On Tuesday noon or night; on Wednesday morn.
70   I prithee name the time, but let it not
Exceed three days. In faith, he's penitent;
And yet his trespass, in our common reason*—   *normal judgment*
Save that, they say, the wars must make example
Out of her* best—is not almost a fault   *(war's)*
75   T' incur a private check.* When shall he come?   *criticism*

Tell me, Othello. I wonder in my soul
What you would ask me that I should deny,
Or stand so mamm'ring on?* What? Michael Cassio, *hesitating*
That came a-wooing with you, and so many a time,
80 When I have spoke of you dispraisingly,
Hath ta'en your part—to have so much to do
To bring him in!* I could do much— *into favor*

OTHELLO   Prithee, no more. Let him come when he will;
I will deny thee nothing.

85 DESDEMONA   Why, this is not a boon!* *favor*
'Tis as I should entreat you wear your gloves,
Or feed on nourishing dishes, or keep you warm,
Or sue to you to do a peculiar* profit *particular*
To your own person. Nay, when I have a suit* *petition*
90 Wherein I mean to touch* your love indeed, *test*
It shall be full of poise* and difficult weight, *balanced judgment*
And fearful to be granted.

OTHELLO   I will deny thee nothing!
Whereon, I do beseech thee, grant me this,
95 To leave me but a little to myself.

DESDEMONA   Shall I deny you? No. Farewell, my lord.

OTHELLO   Farewell, my Desdemona. I'll come to thee straight.* *immediately*

DESDEMONA   Emilia, come.—Be as your fancies teach* you. *lead*
Whate'er you be, I am obedient.

[*Desdemona and Emilia exit.*]

100 OTHELLO   Excellent wretch!* Perdition catch my soul *(affectionate)*
But I do love thee! And when I love thee not,
Chaos is come again.

IAGO   My noble lord—

OTHELLO   What dost thou say, Iago?

105 IAGO   Did Michael Cassio,
When you wooed my lady, know of your love?

OTHELLO   He did, from first to last. Why dost thou ask?

IAGO   But for a satisfaction of my thought,
No further harm.

110 OTHELLO   Why of thy thought, Iago?

IAGO   I did not think he had been acquainted with her.

OTHELLO   O yes, and went between us very oft.

IAGO   Indeed?

OTHELLO   Indeed? Ay, indeed! Discern'st thou aught in that?
115 Is he not honest?*   *honorable*

IAGO   Honest, my lord?

OTHELLO   Honest—ay, honest.

IAGO   My lord, for aught I know.

OTHELLO   What dost thou think?

120 IAGO   Think, my lord?

OTHELLO   "Think, my lord?" By heaven, thou echo'st me
As if there were some monster in thy thought
Too hideous to be shown. Thou dost mean something.
I heard thee say even now, thou lik'st not that,
125 When Cassio left my wife. What didst not like?
And when I told thee he was of my counsel*   *in my confidence*
In my whole course of wooing, thou cried'st "Indeed?"

And didst contract and purse thy brow together
As if thou then hadst shut up in thy brain
130   Some horrible conceit. If thou dost love me,
Show me thy thought.

IAGO   My lord, you know I love you.

OTHELLO   I think thou dost;
And for I know thou 'rt full of love and honesty
135   And weigh'st thy words before thou giv'st them breath,
Therefore these stops* of thine fright me the more.   *pauses*
For such things in a false, disloyal knave
Are tricks of custom;* but in a man that's just,   *habitual*
They're close dilations* working from the heart   *involuntary hesitations*
140   That passion cannot rule.*   *control*

IAGO   For Michael Cassio,
I dare be sworn I think that he is honest.

OTHELLO   I think so too.

IAGO   Men should be what they seem;
145   Or those that be not, would they might seem none!

OTHELLO   Certain, men should be what they seem.

IAGO   Why then, I think Cassio's an honest man.

OTHELLO   Nay, yet there's more in this.
I prithee speak to me as to thy thinkings,
150   As thou dost ruminate, and give thy worst of thoughts
The worst of words.

IAGO   Good my lord, pardon me.
Though I am bound to every act of duty,
I am not bound to that all slaves are free to.*   *(hide their thoughts)*
155   Utter my thoughts? Why, say they are vile and false—
As where's that palace whereinto foul things

Sometimes intrude not? Who has that breast so pure
But some uncleanly apprehensions*   *impure thoughts
Keep leets and law days* and in sessions sit   *hold court
160 With meditations lawful?

OTHELLO   Thou dost conspire against thy friend,* Iago,   *(Othello)
If thou but think'st him wronged and mak'st his ear
A stranger to thy thoughts.

IAGO   I do beseech you,
165 Though I perchance am vicious* in my guess—   *mistaken
As, I confess, it is my nature's plague
To spy into abuses, and oft my jealousy*   *suspicion
Shapes* faults that are not—that your wisdom   *Imagines
From one that so imperfectly conceits
170 Would take no notice, nor build yourself a trouble
Out of his scattering* and unsure observance.   *incoherent
It were not* for your quiet nor your good,   *It would not be good
Nor for my manhood, honesty, and wisdom,
To let you know my thoughts.

175 OTHELLO   What dost thou mean?

IAGO   Good name in man and woman, dear my lord,
Is the immediate jewel of their souls.
Who steals my purse steals trash. 'Tis something, nothing;
'Twas mine, 'tis his, and has been slave to thousands.
180 But he that filches from me my good name
Robs me of that which not enriches him
And makes me poor indeed.

OTHELLO   By heaven, I'll know thy thoughts.

IAGO   You cannot, if my heart were in your hand,
185 Nor shall not, whilst 'tis in my custody.

OTHELLO   Ha?

Jealousy

IAGO   O, beware, my lord, of jealousy!
It is the green-eyed monster which doth mock
The meat it feeds on. That cuckold lives in bliss
190   Who, certain of his fate,* loves not his wronger;*   *(cuckolded) | unfaithful wife*
But O, what damnèd minutes tells he o'er*   *does he count*
Who dotes, yet doubts; suspects, yet strongly loves!

OTHELLO   O misery!

IAGO   Poor and content is rich, and rich enough;
195   But riches fineless* is as poor as winter   *unlimited*
To him that ever fears he shall be poor.
Good God, the souls of all my tribe defend
From jealousy!

OTHELLO   Why, why is this?
200   Think'st thou I'd make a life of jealousy,
To follow still the changes of the moon
With fresh suspicions? No. To be once in doubt
Is once to be resolved.* Exchange me for a goat   *finally settled*
When I shall turn the business of my soul
205   To such exsufflicate and blown* surmises,   *inflated and blown up*
Matching thy inference.* 'Tis not to make me jealous   *implication*
To say my wife is fair, feeds well, loves company,
Is free of speech, sings, plays, and dances well.
Where virtue is, these are more virtuous.
210   Nor from mine own weak merits will I draw
The smallest fear or doubt of her revolt,*   *worry of her inconstancy*
For she had eyes, and chose me. No, Iago,
I'll see before I doubt; when I doubt, prove;
And on the proof, there is no more but this:
215   Away at once with love or jealousy.

IAGO   I am glad of this, for now I shall have reason
To show the love and duty that I bear you
With franker spirit. Therefore, as I am bound,
Receive it from me. I speak not yet of proof.
220   Look to your wife; observe her well with Cassio;

Wear your eyes thus, not jealous nor secure.
I would not have your free and noble nature,
Out of self-bounty,* be abused. Look to 't.   *inherent goodness
I know our country disposition well.
225 In Venice they do let God see the pranks
They dare not show their husbands. Their best conscience
Is not to leave 't undone, but keep 't unknown.

OTHELLO   Dost thou say so?

IAGO   She did deceive her father, marrying you,
230 And when she seemed to shake and fear your looks,
She loved them most.

OTHELLO   And so she did.

IAGO   Why, go to,* then!   *that's it
She that, so young, could give out such a seeming,
235 To seel* her father's eyes up close as oak,   *close
He thought 'twas witchcraft! But I am much to blame.
I humbly do beseech you of your pardon
For too much loving you.

OTHELLO   I am bound to thee forever.

240 IAGO   I see this hath a little dashed your spirits.

OTHELLO   Not a jot, not a jot.

IAGO   I' faith, I fear it has.
I hope you will consider what is spoke
Comes from my love. But I do see you're moved.
245 I am to pray you not to strain my speech
To grosser issues* nor to larger reach   *greater conclusions
Than to suspicion.

OTHELLO   I will not.

IAGO   Should you do so, my lord,
250   My speech should fall into such vile success
As my thoughts aim not at. Cassio's my worthy friend.
My lord, I see you're moved.

OTHELLO   No, not much moved.
I do not think but Desdemona's honest.*   *chaste*

255   IAGO   Long live she so! And long live you to think so!

OTHELLO   And yet, how nature erring from itself—

IAGO   Ay, there's the point. As, to be bold with you,
Not to affect* many proposèd matches   *desire*
Of her own clime, complexion, and degree,*   *rank*
260   Whereto we see in all things nature tends—
Foh! One may smell in such a will* most rank,   *desire*
Foul disproportion,* thoughts unnatural—   *abnormalities*
But pardon me—I do not in position*   *establishing this proposition*
Distinctly speak of her, though I may fear
265   Her will, recoiling* to her better judgment,   *returning*
May fall to match you with her country forms*   *countrymen*
And happily* repent.   *perhaps*

OTHELLO   Farewell, farewell!
If more thou dost perceive, let me know more.
270   Set on thy wife to observe. Leave me, Iago.

IAGO   [*beginning to exit*] My lord, I take my leave.

OTHELLO   Why did I marry? This honest creature doubtless
Sees and knows more, much more, than he unfolds.

IAGO   [*returning*] My lord, I would I might entreat your Honor
275   To scan this thing no farther. Leave it to time.
Although 'tis fit that Cassio have his place—
For sure he fills it up with great ability—
Yet, if you please to hold him off awhile,

You shall by that perceive him and his means.*   (regaining his position)
280 Note if your lady strain his entertainment*   insist upon his reinstatement
With any strong or vehement importunity.
Much will be seen in that. In the meantime,
Let me be thought too busy* in my fears—   meddlesome
As worthy cause I have to fear I am—
285 And hold her free,* I do beseech your Honor.   believe her as guiltless

OTHELLO   Fear not my government.*   self-conduct

IAGO   I once more take my leave.   [*He exits.*]

OTHELLO   This fellow's of exceeding honesty,
And knows all qualities with a learnèd spirit
290 Of human dealings. If I do prove her haggard,*   wild; unchaste
Though that her jesses* were my dear heartstrings,   (trained hawk's leg straps)
I'd whistle her off and let her down the wind
To prey at fortune.* Haply, for* I am black   fend for herself / Perhaps because
And have not those soft parts of* conversation*   easy / manner
295 That chamberers* have, or for I am declined   gallants
Into the vale* of years—yet that's not much—   valley
She's gone, I am abused,* and my relief   deceived
Must be to loathe her. O curse of marriage,
That we can call these delicate creatures ours
300 And not their appetites! I had rather be a toad
And live upon the vapor of a dungeon
Than keep a corner in the thing I love
For others' uses. Yet 'tis the plague of great ones;
Prerogatived* are they less than the base.*   Privileged / lowborn
305 'Tis destiny unshunnable, like death.
Even then this forkèd plague* is fated to us   wearing cuckold's horns
When we do quicken.* Look where she comes.   are conceived
[*Enter Desdemona and Emilia.*]
If she be false, heaven mocks itself!
I'll not believe 't.

310 DESDEMONA   How now, my dear Othello?
Your dinner, and the generous* islanders   noble
By you invited, do attend* your presence.   wait for

OTHELLO   I am to blame.

DESDEMONA   Why do you speak so faintly? Are you not well?

315 OTHELLO   I have a pain upon my forehead, here.*   *(from cuckold's horns)*

DESDEMONA   Faith, that's with watching.* 'Twill away again.   *from lack of sleep*
Let me but bind it hard; within this hour
It will be well.

OTHELLO   Your napkin* is too little.   *handkerchief*
320 Let it alone.   [*The handkerchief falls, unnoticed.*]
        Come, I'll go in with you.

DESDEMONA   I am very sorry that you are not well.

[*Othello and Desdemona exit.*]

EMILIA   [*picking up the handkerchief*]
I am glad I have found this napkin.
This was her first remembrance from the Moor.
325 My wayward husband hath a hundred times
Wooed me to steal it. But she so loves the token
(For he conjured* her she should ever keep it)   *implored*
That she reserves it evermore about her
To kiss and talk to. I'll have the work ta'en out*   *embroidery copied*
330 And give 't Iago. What he will do with it
Heaven knows, not I.
I nothing but to please his fantasy.*   *whim*

[*Enter Iago.*]

IAGO   How now? What do you here alone?

EMILIA   Do not you chide. I have a thing for you.

335 IAGO   You have a thing for me? It is a common thing—

EMILIA   Ha?

IAGO   To have a foolish wife.

EMILIA   O, is that all? What will you give me now
For that same handkerchief?

340   IAGO   What handkerchief?

EMILIA   What handkerchief?
Why, that the Moor first gave to Desdemona,
That which so often you did bid me steal.

IAGO   Hast stol'n it from her?

345   EMILIA   No, faith, she let it drop by negligence,
And to th' advantage* I, being here, took 't up.   *fortunately*
Look, here 'tis.

IAGO   A good wench! Give it me.

EMILIA   What will you do with 't, that you have been so earnest
350   To have me filch it?

IAGO   [*snatching it*] Why, what is that to you?

EMILIA   If it be not for some purpose of import,*   *important purpose*
Give 't me again. Poor lady, she'll run mad
When she shall lack it.

355   IAGO   Be not acknown on 't.*   *Hide your role in it*
I have use for it. Go, leave me.
[*Emilia exits.*]
I will in Cassio's lodging lose this napkin
And let him find it. Trifles light as air
Are to the jealous confirmations strong
360   As proofs of holy writ. This may do something.
The Moor already changes with my poison;
Dangerous conceits* are in their natures poisons,   *ideas*
Which at the first are scarce found to distaste,
But with a little* act upon the blood   *(time)*

365 Burn like the mines of sulfur.
[*Enter Othello.*]

I did say so.

Look where he comes. Not poppy* nor mandragora — *opium*
Nor all the drowsy* syrups of the world — *sleep-inducing*
Shall ever medicine thee to that sweet sleep
370 Which thou owedst* yesterday. — *owned*

OTHELLO   Ha, ha, false to me?

IAGO   Why, how now, general? No more of that!

OTHELLO   Avaunt!* Begone! Thou hast set me on the rack.* — *Leave me / torture device*
I swear 'tis better to be much abused* — *deceived*
375 Than but to know 't a little.

IAGO   How now, my lord?

OTHELLO   What sense had I of her stol'n hours of lust?
I saw 't not, thought it not; it harmed not me.
I slept the next night well, fed well, was free and merry.
380 I found not Cassio's kisses on her lips.
He that is robbed, not wanting* what is stol'n, — *missing*
Let him not know 't, and he's not robbed at all.

IAGO   I am sorry to hear this.

OTHELLO   I had been happy if the general camp,* — *whole army*
385 Pioners* and all, had tasted her sweet body, — *Trench diggers*
So* I had nothing known. O, now, forever — *If*
Farewell the tranquil mind! Farewell content!
Farewell the plumèd troops and the big wars
That makes ambition virtue! O, farewell!
390 Farewell the neighing steed and the shrill trump,* — *trumpet*
The spirit-stirring drum, th' ear-piercing fife,
The royal banner, and all quality,* — *merit*
Pride, pomp, and circumstance of glorious war!
And O you mortal engines,* whose rude throats — *deadly canons*

97

395 Th' immortal Jove's dread clamors* counterfeit, *thunderbolts*
Farewell! Othello's occupation's gone!

IAGO   Is 't possible, my lord?

OTHELLO   Villain, be sure thou prove my love a whore!
Be sure of it. Give me the ocular proof,
400 Or, by the worth of mine eternal soul,
Thou hadst been better have been born a dog
Than answer my waked wrath.

IAGO   Is 't come to this?

OTHELLO   Make me to see 't, or at the least so prove it
405 That the probation* bear no hinge nor loop *proof*
To hang a doubt on, or woe upon thy life!

IAGO   My noble lord—

OTHELLO   If thou dost slander her and torture me,
Never pray more. Abandon all remorse;
410 On horror's head horrors accumulate;
Do deeds to make heaven weep, all Earth amazed;* *astounded*
For nothing canst thou to damnation add
Greater than that.

IAGO   O grace! O heaven forgive me!
415 Are you a man? Have you a soul or sense?
God b' wi' you.* Take mine office.—O wretched fool,* *Goodbye | (to himself)*
That liv'st to make thine honesty a vice!*— *fault*
O monstrous world! Take note, take note, O world:
To be direct and honest is not safe.—
420 I thank you for this profit,* and from hence *profitable lesson*
I'll love no friend, sith* love breeds such offense. *since*

OTHELLO   Nay, stay. Thou shouldst be honest.

IAGO   I should be wise; for honesty's a fool
And loses that* it works for. *what*

OTHELLO   By the world,
425 I think my wife be honest* and think she is not.   *chaste*
I think that thou art just and think thou art not.
I'll have some proof! Her name, that was as fresh
As Dian's* visage, is now begrimed and black   *Diana's (goddess of chastity)*
430 As mine own face. If there be cords, or knives,
Poison, or fire, or suffocating streams,
I'll not endure it. Would I were satisfied!

IAGO   I see you are eaten up with passion.
I do repent me that I put it to you.
435 You would be satisfied?

OTHELLO   Would? Nay, and I will.

IAGO   And may; but how? How satisfied, my lord?
Would you, the supervisor,* grossly gape on,   *spectator*
Behold her topped?*   *sexually mounted*

440 OTHELLO   Death and damnation! O!

IAGO   It were a tedious* difficulty, I think,   *disagreeable*
To bring them to that prospect.* Damn them then   *viewable position*
If ever mortal eyes do see them bolster*   *copulate*
More than their own! What then? How then?
445 What shall I say? Where's satisfaction?
It is impossible you should see this,
Were they as prime* as goats, as hot as monkeys,   *lustful*
As salt as wolves in pride,* and fools as gross   *heat*
As ignorance made drunk. But yet I say,
450 If imputation and strong circumstances*   *circumstantial evidence*
Which lead directly to the door of truth
Will give you satisfaction, you might have 't.

OTHELLO   Give me a living* reason she's disloyal.   *legitimate*

IAGO   I do not like the office,*   *duty*
455 But sith* I am entered in this cause so far,   *since*
Pricked to* 't by foolish honesty and love,   *Prodded on*

I will go on. I lay with Cassio lately,
And being troubled with a raging tooth
I could not sleep. There are a kind of men
460 So loose of soul that in their sleeps will mutter
Their affairs. One of this kind is Cassio.
In sleep I heard him say "Sweet Desdemona,
Let us be wary, let us hide our loves."
And then, sir, would he gripe* and wring my hand, *grip*
465 Cry "O sweet creature!" then kiss me hard,
As if he plucked up kisses by the roots
That grew upon my lips; then laid his leg
O'er my thigh, and sighed, and kissed, and then
Cried "Cursèd fate that gave thee to the Moor!"

470 OTHELLO   O monstrous! Monstrous!

IAGO   Nay, this was but his dream.

OTHELLO   But this denoted a foregone conclusion.*   *earlier event*
'Tis a shrewd doubt,* though it be but a dream.   *reasonable fear*

IAGO   And this may help to thicken other proofs
475 That do demonstrate thinly.

OTHELLO   I'll tear her all to pieces.

IAGO   Nay, but be wise. Yet we see nothing done.
She may be honest yet. Tell me but this:
Have you not sometimes seen a handkerchief
480 Spotted with strawberries in your wife's hand?

OTHELLO   I gave her such a one. 'Twas my first gift.

IAGO   I know not that; but such a handkerchief—
I am sure it was your wife's—did I today
See Cassio wipe his beard with.

485 OTHELLO   If it be that—

Handkerchief

IAGO   If it be that, or any that was hers,
It speaks against her with the other proofs.

OTHELLO   O, that the slave* had forty thousand lives!   *(Cassio)*
One is too poor, too weak for my revenge.
490   Now do I see 'tis true. Look here, Iago,
All my fond love thus do I blow to heaven.
'Tis gone.
Arise, black vengeance, from the hollow hell!
Yield up, O love, thy crown and hearted throne*   *rule of the heart*
495   To tyrannous hate! Swell, bosom, with thy fraught,*   *burden*
For 'tis of aspics'* tongues!   *poisonous snakes'*

IAGO   Yet be content.

OTHELLO   O, blood, blood, blood!

IAGO   Patience, I say. Your mind perhaps may change.

500   OTHELLO   Never, Iago. Like to the Pontic Sea,*   *Black Sea*
Whose icy current and compulsive course
Ne'er feels retiring ebb, but keeps due on
To the Propontic and the Hellespont,
Even so my bloody thoughts, with violent pace
505   Shall ne'er look back, ne'er ebb to humble love,
Till that a capable* and wide revenge   *capacious*
Swallow them up. [*Othello kneels.*] Now by yond marble heaven,
In the due reverence of a sacred vow,
I here engage* my words.   *pledge*

510   IAGO   Do not rise yet.   [*Iago kneels.*]
Witness, you ever-burning lights above,
You elements that clip* us round about,   *embrace*
Witness that here Iago doth give up
The execution* of his wit, hands, heart   *command*
515   To wronged Othello's service! Let him command,
And to obey shall be in me remorse,*   *pity*
What bloody business ever.   [*They rise.*]

OTHELLO   I greet thy love
Not with vain thanks but with acceptance bounteous,
520   And will upon the instant put thee to 't.*   *immediately test it*
Within these three days let me hear thee say
That Cassio's not alive.

IAGO   My friend is dead.
'Tis done at your request. But let her live.

525   OTHELLO   Damn her, lewd minx! O, damn her, damn her!
Come, go with me apart. I will withdraw
To furnish me with some swift means of death
For the fair devil. Now art thou my lieutenant.

IAGO   I am your own forever.

[*They exit.*]

Scene 4.
Before the citadel

[Enter Desdemona, Emilia, and Clown.]

DESDEMONA Do you know, sirrah, where Lieutenant Cassio lies?

CLOWN I dare not say he lies anywhere.

DESDEMONA Why, man?

CLOWN He's a soldier, and for me to say a soldier lies, 'tis stabbing.

5 DESDEMONA Go to! Where lodges he?

CLOWN To tell you where he lodges is to tell you where I lie.

DESDEMONA Can anything be made of this?

CLOWN I know not where he lodges; and for me to devise a lodging and say he lies here, or he lies there, were to lie in mine own throat.

10 DESDEMONA Can you inquire him out, and be edified* by report?   *instructed*

CLOWN I will catechize the world for him—that is, make questions, and by them answer.*   *find answers*

DESDEMONA Seek him, bid him come hither. Tell him I have moved*   *petitioned*
my lord on his behalf and hope all will be well.

15 CLOWN To do this is within the compass* of man's wit, and   *scope*
therefore I will attempt the doing it.   *[Clown exits.]*

DESDEMONA Where should I lose that handkerchief, Emilia?

EMILIA   I know not, madam.

DESDEMONA   Believe me, I had rather have lost my purse
20 Full of crusadoes.* And but* my noble Moor   *gold coins | but that*
Is true of mind and made of no such baseness
As jealous creatures are, it were enough
To put him to ill thinking.

EMILIA   Is he not jealous?

25 DESDEMONA   Who, he? I think the sun where he was born
Drew all such humors* from him.   *(bodily fluids determining temperament)*

EMILIA   Look where he comes.

[*Enter Othello.*]

DESDEMONA   I will not leave him now till Cassio
Be called to him.—How is 't with you, my lord?

30 OTHELLO   Well, my good lady. [*Aside*] O, hardness to dissemble!—
How do you, Desdemona?

DESDEMONA   Well, my good lord.

OTHELLO   Give me your hand.   [*He takes her hand.*]
This hand is moist,* my lady.   *(sign of carnal desire)*

35 DESDEMONA   It yet has felt no age nor known no sorrow.

OTHELLO   This argues fruitfulness and liberal heart.
Hot, hot, and moist. This hand of yours requires
A sequester from liberty, fasting and prayer,
Much castigation, exercise devout;
40 For here's a young and sweating devil here
That commonly rebels. 'Tis a good hand,
A frank* one.   *(sexually) open*

DESDEMONA   You may indeed say so,
For 'twas that hand that gave away my heart.

45 OTHELLO   A liberal hand! The hearts of old gave hands,
But our new heraldry is hands, not hearts.

DESDEMONA   I cannot speak of this. Come now, your promise.

OTHELLO   What promise, chuck?*   *(affectionate)*

DESDEMONA   I have sent to bid Cassio come speak with you.

50 OTHELLO   I have a salt and sorry rheum* offends me.   *watering eyes*
Lend me thy handkerchief.

DESDEMONA   Here, my lord.

OTHELLO   That which I gave you.

DESDEMONA   I have it not about me.

55 OTHELLO   Not?

DESDEMONA   No, faith, my lord.

OTHELLO   That's a fault. That handkerchief
Did an Egyptian to my mother give.
She was a charmer,* and could almost read   *sorceress*
60 The thoughts of people. She told her, while she kept it,
'Twould make her amiable* and subdue my father   *desirable*
Entirely to her love. But if she lost it,
Or made a gift of it, my father's eye
Should hold her loathèd, and his spirits should hunt
65 After new fancies. She, dying, gave it me,
And bid me, when my fate would have me wived,
To give it her.* I did so; and take heed on 't,   *to my wife*
Make it a darling like your precious eye.
To lose 't or give 't away were such perdition*   *loss*
70 As nothing else could match.

DESDEMONA   Is 't possible?

OTHELLO   'Tis true. There's magic in the web of it.
A sybil* that had numbered in the world   *female prophet*
The sun to course two hundred compasses,*   *two hundred years old*
75 In her prophetic fury sewed the work.
The worms were hallowed that did breed the silk,
And it was dyed in mummy, which the skillful
Conserved of* maidens' hearts.   *Prepared from*

DESDEMONA   I' faith, is 't true?

80 OTHELLO   Most veritable. Therefore, look to 't well.

DESDEMONA   Then would to God that I had never seen 't!

OTHELLO   Ha? Wherefore?

DESDEMONA   Why do you speak so startingly* and rash?   *impetuously*

OTHELLO   Is 't lost? Is 't gone? Speak, is 't out o' th' way?*   *missing*

85 DESDEMONA   Heaven bless us!

OTHELLO   Say you?

DESDEMONA   It is not lost, but what an if it were?

OTHELLO   How?

DESDEMONA   I say it is not lost.

90 OTHELLO   Fetch 't. Let me see 't!

DESDEMONA   Why, so I can. But I will not now.
This is a trick to put me from my suit.
Pray you, let Cassio be received again.

OTHELLO   Fetch me the handkerchief! [*Aside*] My mind misgives.

DESDEMONA   Come, come.
You'll never meet a more sufficient* man.   *capable

OTHELLO   The handkerchief!

DESDEMONA   I pray, talk me of Cassio.

OTHELLO   The handkerchief!

DESDEMONA   A man that all his time
Hath founded his good fortunes on your love;
Shared dangers with you—

OTHELLO   The handkerchief!

DESDEMONA   I' faith, you are to blame.

OTHELLO   Zounds!   [*He exits.*]

EMILIA   Is not this man jealous?

DESDEMONA   I ne'er saw this before.
Sure, there's some wonder in this handkerchief!
I am most unhappy in the loss of it.

EMILIA   'Tis not a year or two shows us a man.
They are all but* stomachs, and we all but food;   *nothing but
They eat us hungerly, and when they are full
They belch us.
[*Enter Iago and Cassio.*]
                        Look you—Cassio and my husband.

IAGO   [*to Cassio*] There is no other way; 'tis she must do 't,
And, lo, the happiness!* Go and importune her.   *happy coincidence

DESDEMONA   How now, good Cassio, what's the news with you?

CASSIO   Madam, my former suit. I do beseech you
That by your virtuous means I may again

120 Exist, and be a member of his love
Whom I with all the office of my heart
Entirely honor. I would not be delayed.
If my offense be of such mortal* kind   *deadly*
That nor* my service past nor present sorrows   *Neither*
125 Nor purposed* merit in futurity*   *intended | the future*
Can ransom me into his love again,
But to know so must be my benefit.
So shall I clothe me in a forced content,
And shut myself up in* some other course   *limit myself*
130 To fortune's alms.

DESDEMONA   Alas, thrice-gentle Cassio,
My advocation is not now in tune.*   *isn't working*
My lord is not my lord; nor should I know him
Were he in favor as in humor altered.
135 So help me every spirit sanctified
As I have spoken for you all my best,
And stood within the blank of* his displeasure   *in target of*
For my free speech! You must awhile be patient.
What I can do I will; and more I will
140 Than for myself I dare. Let that suffice you.

IAGO   Is my lord angry?

EMILIA   He went hence but now,
And certainly in strange unquietness.

IAGO   Can he be angry? I have seen the cannon
145 When it hath blown his ranks into the air
And, like the devil, from his very arm
Puffed* his own brother—and is he angry?   *Blown up*
Something of moment* then. I will go meet him.   *importance*
There's matter in 't indeed if he be angry.

150 DESDEMONA   I prithee do so.
[*Iago exits.*]
Something, sure, of state,*   *state business*
Either from Venice, or some unhatched practice*   *undisclosed plot*

Made demonstrable* here in Cyprus to him, *Revealed*
Hath puddled* his clear spirit; and in such cases *dirtied*
155 Men's natures wrangle with inferior things,
Though great ones are their object. 'Tis even so.
For let our finger ache, and it endues* *brings*
Our other healthful members even to a sense
Of pain. Nay, we must think men are not gods,
160 Nor of them look for such observancy* *attention*
As fits the bridal.* Beshrew* me much, Emilia, *wedding / (curse)*
I was—unhandsome* warrior as I am!— *unskilled*
Arraigning his unkindness with my soul.
But now I find I had suborned the witness,
165 And he's indicted falsely.

EMILIA   Pray heaven it be
State matters, as you think, and no conception
Nor no jealous toy* concerning you. *whim*

DESDEMONA   Alas the day, I never gave him cause!

170 EMILIA   But jealous souls will not be answered so.
They are not ever jealous for the cause,
But jealous for they're jealous. It is a monster
Begot upon itself, born on itself.

DESDEMONA   Heaven keep that monster from Othello's mind!

175 EMILIA   Lady, amen.

DESDEMONA   I will go seek him.—Cassio, walk hereabout.
If I do find him fit, I'll move your suit
And seek to effect it to my uttermost.

CASSIO   I humbly thank your Ladyship.

[*Desdemona and Emilia exit.
Enter Bianca.*]

180   BIANCA   'Save you,* friend Cassio!   *God save you*

CASSIO   What make* you from home?   *brings*
How is 't with you, my most fair Bianca?
I' faith, sweet love, I was coming to your house.

BIANCA   And I was going to your lodging, Cassio.
185   What, keep a week away? Seven days and nights,
Eightscore eight hours, and lovers' absent hours
More tedious than the dial eightscore times?
O weary reck'ning!*   *calculating*

CASSIO   Pardon me, Bianca.
190   I have this while with leaden thoughts been pressed,
But I shall in a more continuate* time   *opportune*
Strike off this score of absence. Sweet Bianca,
[*Giving her Desdemona's handkerchief.*]
Take me this work out.*   *Copy this pattern*

BIANCA   O, Cassio, whence came this?
195   This is some token from a newer friend.
To the felt absence now I feel a cause.
Is 't come to this? Well, well.

CASSIO   Go to,* woman!   *Stop it*
Throw your vile guesses in the devil's teeth,
200   From whence you have them. You are jealous now
That this is from some mistress, some remembrance.
No, by my faith, Bianca.

BIANCA   Why, whose is it?

CASSIO   I know not neither. I found it in my chamber.
205   I like the work well. Ere it be demanded,*   *sought out*
As like* enough it will, I would have it copied.   *likely*
Take it, and do 't, and leave me for this time.

BIANCA   Leave you? Wherefore?

CASSIO   I do attend here on the General,
210   And think it no addition,* nor my wish,   *(to my cause)*
To have him see me womaned.*   *with a woman*

BIANCA   Why, I pray you?

CASSIO   Not that I love you not.

BIANCA   But that you do not love me!
215   I pray you bring me on the way a little,
And say if I shall see you soon at night.

CASSIO   'Tis but a little way that I can bring you,
For I attend here. But I'll see you soon.

BIANCA   'Tis very good. I must be circumstanced.*   *content with the circumstances*

[*They exit.*]

Act 4.

Scene 1.
Before the citadel

[Enter Othello and Iago.]

IAGO   Will you think so?

OTHELLO   Think so, Iago?

IAGO   What,
To kiss in private?

5   OTHELLO   An unauthorized kiss!

IAGO   Or to be naked with her friend in bed
An hour or more, not meaning any harm?

OTHELLO   Naked in bed, Iago, and not mean harm?
It is hypocrisy against the devil!
10   They that mean virtuously, and yet do so,
The devil their virtue tempts, and they tempt heaven.

IAGO   If they do nothing, 'tis a venial slip.*   *excusable sin*
But if I give my wife a handkerchief—

OTHELLO   What then?

15   IAGO   Why then, 'tis hers, my lord, and being hers,
She may, I think, bestow 't on any man.

OTHELLO   She is protectress of her honor, too.
May she give that?

IAGO   Her honor is an essence that's not seen;
They have it very oft that have it* not.   *the reputation for honor
But for the handkerchief—

OTHELLO   By heaven, I would most gladly have forgot it.
Thou saidst—O, it comes o'er my memory
As doth the raven* o'er the infectious* house,   *(ill omen) / *plagued
Boding to all—he had my handkerchief.

IAGO   Ay, what of that?

OTHELLO   That's not so good now.

IAGO   What
If I had said I had seen him do you wrong?
Or heard him say (as knaves be such abroad,
Who having, by their own importunate suit
Or voluntary dotage* of some mistress,   *foolish affection
Convincèd or supplied them,* cannot choose   *satisfied them
But they must blab)—

OTHELLO   Hath he said anything?

IAGO   He hath, my lord, but be you well assured,
No more than he'll unswear.

OTHELLO   What hath he said?

IAGO   Faith, that he did—I know not what he did.

OTHELLO   What? What?

IAGO   Lie—

OTHELLO   With her?

IAGO   With her—on her—what you will.

OTHELLO   Lie with her? Lie on her? We say "lie on her"* when they

45 belie* her. Lie with her—Zounds, that's fulsome!* Handkerchief—

confessions—handkerchief. To confess and be hanged for his labor.

First to be hanged and then to confess—I tremble at it. Nature

would not invest herself in such shadowing passion without some

instruction.* It is not words that shakes me thus. Pish! Noses, ears,

50 and lips—is 't possible? Confess—handkerchief—O, devil!

[*He falls into a trance.*]

IAGO   Work on,

My medicine, work! Thus credulous fools are caught,

And many worthy and chaste dames even thus,

All guiltless, meet reproach.—What ho! My lord!

55 My lord, I say. Othello!

[*Enter Cassio.*]

                    How now, Cassio?

CASSIO   What's the matter?

IAGO   My lord is fall'n into an epilepsy.

This is his second fit. He had one yesterday.

60 CASSIO   Rub him about the temples.

IAGO   No, forbear.

The lethargy* must have his* quiet course.

If not, he foams at mouth, and by and by

Breaks out to savage madness. Look, he stirs.

65 Do you withdraw yourself a little while.

He will recover straight.* When he is gone,

I would on great occasion* speak with you.

[*Cassio exits.*]

How is it, general? Have you not hurt your head?

OTHELLO   Dost thou mock me?*

70 IAGO   I mock you not, by heaven!

Would you would bear your fortune* like a man!

Marginal glosses (right column):

- *(sexual)* — line 44
- *slander | obscene* — line 45
- *information* — line 49
- *trance | its* — line 62
- *immediately* — line 66
- *important subject* — line 67
- *(for sprouting cuckold's horns)* — line 69
- *cuckold's fate* — line 71

OTHELLO   A hornèd man's a monster and a beast.

IAGO   There's many a beast, then, in a populous city,
And many a civil* monster.   *city-dwelling

75   OTHELLO   Did he confess it?

IAGO   Good sir, be a man!
Think every bearded fellow that's but yoked*   *married
May draw with you.* There's millions now alive   *face similar fate
That nightly lie in those unproper beds
80   Which they dare swear peculiar.* Your case is better.   *are their own
O, 'tis the spite of hell, the fiend's* arch-mock,   *devil's
To lip* a wanton in a secure couch*   *kiss | *bed free of suspicion
And to suppose her chaste! No, let me know,
And knowing what I am,* I know what she shall be.   *(a cuckold)

85   OTHELLO   O, thou art wise, 'tis certain.

IAGO   Stand you awhile apart.
Confine yourself but in a patient list.*   *boundary
Whilst you were here, o'erwhelmèd with your grief—
A passion most unsuiting such a man—
90   Cassio came hither. I shifted him away
And laid good 'scuses upon your ecstasy,*   *trance
Bade him anon* return and here speak with me,   *soon
The which he promised. Do but encave* yourself,   *Hide
And mark the fleers, the gibes,* and notable scorns   *sneers
95   That dwell in every region of his face.
For I will make him tell the tale anew—
Where, how, how oft, how long ago, and when
He hath and is again to cope* your wife.   *copulate with
I say but mark his gesture. Marry, patience,
100   Or I shall say you're all in all in spleen,*   *impulsive
And nothing of a man.

OTHELLO   Dost thou hear, Iago,
I will be found most cunning in my patience,
But (dost thou hear?) most bloody.

IAGO   That's not amiss.
But yet keep time* in all. Will you withdraw?   *maintain control*
[*Othello withdraws.*]
Now will I question Cassio of Bianca,
A huswife* that by selling her desires   *prostitute*
Buys herself bread and clothes. It is a creature
110 That dotes on Cassio—as 'tis the strumpet's plague
To beguile many and be beguiled by one.
He, when he hears of her, cannot restrain
From the excess of laughter. Here he comes.
[*Enter Cassio.*]
As he shall smile, Othello shall go mad,
115 And his unbookish* jealousy must construe   *naive*
Poor Cassio's smiles, gestures, and light behaviors
Quite in the wrong.—How do you, lieutenant?

CASSIO   The worser that you give me the addition*   *title*
Whose want* even kills me.   *lack*

120 IAGO   Ply Desdemona well, and you are sure on 't.
Now, if this suit lay in Bianca's power,
How quickly should you speed!*   *succeed*

CASSIO   [*laughing*] Alas, poor caitiff!*   *wretch*

OTHELLO   Look how he laughs already!

125 IAGO   I never knew woman love man so.

CASSIO   Alas, poor rogue, I think i' faith she loves me.

OTHELLO   Now he denies it faintly and laughs it out.

IAGO   Do you hear, Cassio?

OTHELLO   Now he importunes him
130 To tell it o'er. Go to, well said, well said.

IAGO   She gives it out that you shall marry her.
Do you intend it?

CASSIO   Ha, ha, ha!

OTHELLO   Do you triumph, Roman? Do you triumph?

135   CASSIO   I marry her? What, a customer?* Prithee bear some charity   *courtesan*
to my wit!* Do not think it so unwholesome.* Ha, ha, ha!   *sense* / *tainted*

OTHELLO   So, so, so, so. They laugh that wins.

IAGO   Faith, the cry* goes that you marry her.   *common talk*

CASSIO   Prithee say true!

140   IAGO   I am a very villain else.

OTHELLO   Have you scored* me? Well.   *wounded*

CASSIO   This is the monkey's own giving out.* She is persuaded   *Bianca's own story*
I will marry her out of her own love and flattery, not out of my promise.

OTHELLO   Iago beckons me. Now he begins the story.

145   CASSIO   She was here even now. She haunts me in every place. I was
the other day talking on the sea-bank with certain Venetians, and
thither comes the bauble.* By this hand, she falls thus about my neck!   *silly woman*

OTHELLO   Crying, "O dear Cassio," as it were; his gesture imports* it.   *indicates*

CASSIO   So hangs and lolls and weeps upon me, so shakes and pulls me.
150   Ha, ha, ha!

OTHELLO   Now he tells how she plucked him to my chamber.—
O, I see that nose of yours, but not that dog I shall throw it to.*   *(envisioning revenge)*

CASSIO   Well, I must leave her company.

IAGO   Before me, look where she comes.

[*Enter Bianca.*]

CASSIO   'Tis such another fitchew*—marry, a perfumed one!—   *prostitute*
What do you mean by this haunting of me?

BIANCA   Let the devil and his dam* haunt you! What did you mean   *mother*
by that same handkerchief you gave me even now? I was a fine fool
to take it! I must take out* the work? A likely piece of work,* that   *copy | story*
you should find it in your chamber and know not who left it there!
This is some minx's token, and I must take out the work! There,
give it your hobbyhorse.* Wheresoever you had it, I'll take out   *mistress*
no work on 't.

CASSIO   How now, my sweet Bianca? How now? How now?

OTHELLO   By heaven, that should* be my handkerchief!   *must*

BIANCA   If you'll come to supper tonight you may. If you will not,
come when you are next prepared for.*   [*She exits.*]   *never*

IAGO   After her, after her!

CASSIO   Faith, I must. She'll rail in the streets else.

IAGO   Will you sup there?

CASSIO   Faith, I intend so.

IAGO   Well, I may chance to see you, for I would very fain* speak   *be pleased to*
with you.

CASSIO   Prithee come. Will you?

IAGO   Go to; say no more.   [*Cassio exits.*]

OTHELLO   [*coming forward*] How shall I murder him, Iago?

IAGO   Did you perceive how he laughed at his vice?

OTHELLO   O Iago!

IAGO   And did you see the handkerchief?

180 OTHELLO   Was that mine?

IAGO   Yours, by this hand! And to see how he prizes* the foolish   *regards
woman your wife! She gave it him, and he hath giv'n it his whore.

OTHELLO   I would have him nine years a-killing! A fine woman,
a fair woman, a sweet woman!

185 IAGO   Nay, you must forget that.

OTHELLO   Ay, let her rot and perish and be damned tonight, for she
shall not live. No, my heart is turned to stone. I strike it, and it hurts
my hand. O, the world hath not a sweeter creature! She might lie by
an emperor's side and command him tasks.

190 IAGO   Nay, that's not your way.*   *(way to think)

OTHELLO   Hang her, I do but say what she is! So delicate with her
needle, an admirable musician—O, she will sing the savageness out
of a bear! Of so high and plenteous wit and invention!*   *imagination

IAGO   She's the worse for all this.

195 OTHELLO   O, a thousand, a thousand times!—And then of so gentle*   *noble
a condition!

IAGO   Ay, too gentle.*   *generous (sexually)

OTHELLO   Nay, that's certain. But yet the pity of it, Iago!
O, Iago, the pity of it, Iago!

200 IAGO   If you are so fond* over her iniquity, give her patent*   *foolish / permission
to offend, for if it touch not you, it comes near* nobody.   *affects

OTHELLO   I will chop her into messes!* Cuckold me?   *pieces*

IAGO   O, 'tis foul in her.

OTHELLO   With mine officer!

205   IAGO   That's fouler.

OTHELLO   Get me some poison, Iago, this night. I'll not expostulate
with her lest her body and beauty unprovide my mind* again.   *weaken my resolve*
This night, Iago.

IAGO   Do it not with poison. Strangle her in her bed, even the bed
210   she hath contaminated.

OTHELLO   Good, good. The justice of it pleases. Very good.

IAGO   And for Cassio, let me be his undertaker.* You shall hear more   *murderer*
by midnight.

OTHELLO   Excellent good.
[*A trumpet sounds.*]
215   What trumpet is that same?

IAGO   I warrant something from Venice.
[*Enter Lodovico, Desdemona, and Attendants.*]
'Tis Lodovico. This comes from the Duke.
See, your wife's with him.

LODOVICO   God save you, worthy general.

220   OTHELLO   With all my heart, sir.

LODOVICO   The Duke and the Senators of Venice greet you.
[*He hands Othello a paper.*]

OTHELLO   I kiss the instrument of their pleasures.*   *commands*

DESDEMONA   And what's the news, good cousin Lodovico?

IAGO   I am very glad to see you, signior.
225   Welcome to Cyprus.

LODOVICO   I thank you. How does Lieutenant Cassio?

IAGO   Lives, sir.

DESDEMONA   Cousin, there's fall'n between him and my lord
An unkind breach, but you shall make all well.

230   OTHELLO   Are you sure of that?

DESDEMONA   My lord?

OTHELLO   [*reading*] "This fail you not to do, as you will"—

LODOVICO   He did not call; he's busy in* the paper.   *with*
Is there division 'twixt my lord and Cassio?

235   DESDEMONA   A most unhappy one. I would do much
T' atone* them, for the love I bear to Cassio.   *reconcile*

OTHELLO   Fire and brimstone!

DESDEMONA   My lord?

OTHELLO   Are you wise?*   *sane*

240   DESDEMONA   What, is he angry?

LODOVICO   May be the letter moved him.
For, as I think, they do command him home,
Deputing Cassio in his government.*   *(Othello's position)*

DESDEMONA   By my troth, I am glad on 't.

245   OTHELLO   Indeed?

DESDEMONA   My lord?

OTHELLO   I am glad to see you mad.*   *crazy*

DESDEMONA   Why, sweet Othello!

OTHELLO   [*striking her*] Devil!

250 DESDEMONA   I have not deserved this.

LODOVICO   My lord, this would not be believed in Venice,
Though I should swear I saw 't. 'Tis very much.*   *serious*
Make her amends. She weeps.

OTHELLO   O, devil, devil!
255 If that the Earth could teem* with woman's tears,   *spawn*
Each drop she falls would prove a crocodile.
Out of my sight!

DESDEMONA   I will not stay to offend you.   [*She begins to leave.*]

LODOVICO   Truly an obedient lady.
260 I do beseech your Lordship call her back.

OTHELLO   Mistress.

DESDEMONA   [*turning back*] My lord?

OTHELLO   What would you with her, sir?

LODOVICO   Who, I, my lord?

265 OTHELLO   Ay, you did wish that I would make her turn.*   *return*
Sir, she can turn, and turn,* and yet go on,   *(sexual)*
And turn again. And she can weep, sir, weep.
And she's obedient, as you say, obedient.
Very obedient.—Proceed you in your tears.—
270 Concerning this, sir—O, well-painted passion!*—   *counterfeit emotion*
I am commanded home.—Get you away.
I'll send for you anon.—Sir, I obey the mandate
And will return to Venice.—Hence, avaunt!*   *begone*

[*Desdemona exits.*]

Cassio shall have my place.* And, sir, tonight   official position

275 I do entreat that we may sup together.

You are welcome, sir, to Cyprus. Goats and monkeys!*   [*He exits.*]   *(symbols of lust)*

LODOVICO   Is this the noble Moor, whom our full senate

Call all in all sufficient? Is this the nature

Whom passion could not shake, whose solid virtue

280 The shot of accident nor dart of chance

Could neither graze nor pierce?

IAGO   He is much changed.

LODOVICO   Are his wits safe? Is he not light of brain?

IAGO   He's that he is. I may not breathe my censure

285 What he might be. If what he might he is not,

I would to heaven he were.

LODOVICO   What? Strike his wife?

IAGO   'Faith, that was not so well. Yet would I knew

That stroke would prove the worst.

290 LODOVICO   Is it his use?*   *custom*

Or did the letters work upon his blood*   *passions*

And new-create this fault?

IAGO   Alas, alas!

It is not honesty in me to speak

295 What I have seen and known. You shall observe him,

And his own courses* will denote him so   *conduct*

That I may save my speech. Do but go after

And mark how he continues.

LODOVICO   I am sorry that I am deceived in him.

[*They exit.*]

Scene 2.
The citadel

[*Enter Othello and Emilia.*]

OTHELLO   You have seen nothing then?

EMILIA   Nor ever heard, nor ever did suspect.

OTHELLO   Yes, you have seen Cassio and she together.

EMILIA   But then I saw no harm, and then I heard
5 Each syllable that breath made up between them.

OTHELLO   What, did they never whisper?

EMILIA   Never, my lord.

OTHELLO   Nor send you out o' th' way?

EMILIA   Never.

10 OTHELLO   To fetch her fan, her gloves, her mask, nor nothing?

EMILIA   Never, my lord.

OTHELLO   That's strange.

EMILIA   I durst,* my lord, to wager she is honest,*   *dare | chaste*
Lay down my soul at stake.* If you think other,   *as my bet*
15 Remove your thought. It doth abuse* your bosom.   *deceive*
If any wretch have put this in your head,
Let heaven requite it with the serpent's curse,
For if she be not honest, chaste, and true,
There's no man happy.* The purest of their wives   *fortunate*
20 Is foul as slander.

OTHELLO   Bid her come hither. Go.   [*Emilia exits.*]
She says enough. Yet she's a simple bawd
That cannot say as much. This is a subtle whore,
A closet lock and key* of villainous secrets.   *hider*
25 And yet she'll kneel and pray. I have seen her do 't.

[*Enter Desdemona and Emilia.*]

DESDEMONA   My lord, what is your will?

OTHELLO   Pray you, chuck,* come hither.   *(affectionate)*

DESDEMONA   What is your pleasure?

OTHELLO   Let me see your eyes. Look in my face.

30 DESDEMONA   What horrible fancy's this?

OTHELLO   [*to Emilia*] Some of your function, mistress.
Leave procreants* alone, and shut the door.   *copulators*
Cough, or cry "hem," if anybody come.
Your mystery,* your mystery! Nay, dispatch.   *trade*

[*Emilia exits.*]

35 DESDEMONA   [*kneeling*] Upon my knees, what doth your speech import?
I understand a fury in your words,
But not the words.

OTHELLO   Why? What art thou?

DESDEMONA   Your wife, my lord, your true and loyal wife.

40 OTHELLO   Come, swear it. Damn thyself,
Lest, being* like one of heaven, the devils themselves   *appearing*
Should fear to seize thee. Therefore be double damned.
Swear thou art honest.

DESDEMONA   Heaven doth truly know it.

OTHELLO   Heaven truly knows that thou art false as hell.

DESDEMONA   [*standing*] To whom, my lord? With whom?
How am I false?

OTHELLO   Ah, Desdemon, away, away, away!

DESDEMONA   Alas the heavy day, why do you weep?
Am I the motive of these tears, my lord?
If haply* you my father do suspect   *perhaps*
An instrument of this your calling back,*   *(to Venice)*
Lay not your blame on me. If you have lost him,
I have lost him too.

OTHELLO   Had it pleased heaven
To try me with affliction, had they* rained   *the heavens*
All kind of sores and shames on my bare head,
Steeped me in poverty to the very lips,
Given to captivity me and my utmost hopes,
I should have found in some place of my soul
A drop of patience. But alas, to make me
A fixèd figure for the time of scorn
To point his slow unmoving finger at—
Yet could I bear that too, well, very well.
But there where I have garnered* up my heart,   *stored*
Where either I must live or bear no life,
The fountain from the which my current runs
Or else dries up—to be discarded thence,
Or keep it as a cistern for foul toads
To knot and gender* in—turn thy complexion there,   *To couple and engender*
Patience, thou young and rose-lipped cherubin,
Ay, there look grim as hell.

DESDEMONA   I hope my noble lord esteems me honest.

OTHELLO   O, ay, as summer flies are in the shambles,*   *slaughterhouse*
That quicken* even with blowing! O thou weed,   *become pregnant*
Who art so lovely fair, and smell'st so sweet
That the sense aches at thee, would thou hadst ne'er been born!

DESDEMONA   Alas, what ignorant* sin have I committed?   *unwitting*

OTHELLO   Was this fair paper, this most goodly book,
80   Made to write "whore" upon? What committed?
Committed? O thou public commoner,*   *prostitute*
I should make very forges of my cheeks
That would to cinders burn up modesty,
Did I but speak thy deeds. What committed?
85   Heaven stops the nose at it, and the moon* winks;   *(Diana, goddess of the moon and chastity)*
The bawdy* wind that kisses all it meets   *promiscuous*
Is hushed within the hollow mine of earth
And will not hear 't. What committed?
Impudent strumpet!

90   DESDEMONA   By heaven, you do me wrong!

OTHELLO   Are not you a strumpet?

DESDEMONA   No, as I am a Christian!
If to preserve this vessel for my lord
From any other foul unlawful touch
95   Be not to be a strumpet, I am none.

OTHELLO   What, not a whore?

DESDEMONA   No, as I shall be saved.

OTHELLO   Is 't possible?

DESDEMONA   O, heaven forgive us!

100   OTHELLO   I cry you mercy,* then.   *beg your pardon*
I took you for that cunning whore of Venice
That married with Othello.—You, mistress,
[*Enter Emilia.*]
That have the office opposite to Saint Peter
And keeps the gate of hell—you, you, ay, you!
105   We have done our course.* There's money for your pains.   *business*

[*He gives Desdemona money.*]
I pray you turn the key and keep our counsel.   [*He exits.*]

EMILIA   Alas, what does this gentleman conceive?*   *believe*
How do you, madam? How do you, my good lady?

DESDEMONA   Faith, half asleep.

110   EMILIA   Good madam, what's the matter with my lord?

DESDEMONA   With who?

EMILIA   Why, with my lord, madam.

DESDEMONA   Who is thy lord?

EMILIA   He that is yours, sweet lady.

115   DESDEMONA   I have none. Do not talk to me, Emilia.
I cannot weep, nor answers have I none
But what should go by water.* Prithee, tonight   *be said in tears*
Lay on my bed my wedding sheets. Remember.
And call thy husband hither.

120   EMILIA   Here's a change indeed.   [*She exits.*]

DESDEMONA   'Tis meet* I should be used so, very meet.   *fitting*
How have I been behaved that he might stick
The small'st opinion on my least misuse?*   *smallest fault*

[*Enter Iago and Emilia.*]

IAGO   What is your pleasure, madam? How is 't with you?

125   DESDEMONA   I cannot tell. Those that do teach young babes
Do it with gentle means and easy tasks.
He might have chid me so, for, in good faith,
I am a child to chiding.*   *new to being chided*

IAGO   What is the matter, lady?

130 EMILIA   Alas, Iago, my lord hath so bewhored her,*   *called her a whore
      Thrown such despite* and heavy terms upon her   *contempt
      As true hearts cannot bear.

      DESDEMONA   Am I that name, Iago?

      IAGO   What name, fair lady?

135 DESDEMONA   Such as she said my lord did say I was.

      EMILIA   He called her "whore." A beggar in his drink
      Could not have laid such terms upon his callet.*   *whore

      IAGO   Why did he so?

      DESDEMONA   I do not know. I am sure I am none such.

140 IAGO   Do not weep, do not weep! Alas the day!

      EMILIA   Hath she forsook so many noble matches,
      Her father and her country and her friends,
      To be called "whore"? Would it not make one weep?

      DESDEMONA   It is my wretched fortune.

145 IAGO   Beshrew* him for 't! How comes this trick* upon him?   *Curse / foolishness

      DESDEMONA   Nay, heaven doth know.

      EMILIA   I will be hanged if some eternal villain,
      Some busy* and insinuating rogue,   *meddlesome
      Some cogging,* cozening* slave, to get some office,   *fraudulent / deceiving
150 Have not devised this slander. I will be hanged else.

      IAGO   Fie, there is no such man. It is impossible.

DESDEMONA   If any such there be, heaven pardon him.

EMILIA   A halter* pardon him, and hell gnaw his bones!   *hangman's noose
Why should he call her "whore"? Who keeps her company?
155   What place? What time? What form? What likelihood?
The Moor's abused* by some most villainous knave,   *deceived
Some base notorious knave, some scurvy fellow.
O heaven, that* such companions thou 'dst unfold,*   *would that / reveal
And put in every honest hand a whip
160   To lash the rascals naked through the world,
Even from the east to th' west!

IAGO   Speak within door.*   *more temperately

EMILIA   O, fie upon them! Some such squire* he was   *fellow
That turned your wit the seamy side without*   *inside out
165   And made you to suspect me with the Moor.

IAGO   You are a fool. Go to!

DESDEMONA   Alas, Iago,
What shall I do to win my lord again?
Good friend, go to him. For by this light of heaven,
170   I know not how I lost him. [She kneels.] Here I kneel.
If e'er my will did trespass 'gainst his love,
Either in discourse* of thought or actual deed,   *course
Or that mine eyes, mine ears, or any sense
Delighted them in any other form,*   *anyone but him
175   Or that I do not yet,* and ever did,   *still
And ever will—though he do shake me off
To beggarly divorcement—love him dearly,
Comfort forswear me!* [She stands.] Unkindness may do much,   *forsake me
And his unkindness may defeat my life,
180   But never taint my love. I cannot say "whore"—
It does abhor me now I speak the word.
To do the act that might the addition* earn,   *name
Not the world's mass of vanity* could make me.   *worldly pleasure

133

IAGO   I pray you be content. 'Tis but his humor.*   *mood
185 The business of the state does him offense,
And he does chide with you.

DESDEMONA   If 'twere no other—

IAGO   It is but so, I warrant.
[*Trumpets sound.*]
Hark how these instruments summon to supper.
190 The messengers of Venice stays the meat.*   *are waiting to eat
Go in and weep not. All things shall be well.
[*Desdemona and Emilia exit.*
Enter Roderigo.]
How now, Roderigo?

RODERIGO   I do not find
That thou deal'st justly with me.

195 IAGO   What in the contrary?

RODERIGO   Every day thou daff'st me* with some device,* Iago,   *make me a fool / trick
and rather, as it seems to me now, keep'st from me all conveniency*   *occasion
than suppliest me with the least advantage of hope. I will indeed
no longer endure it. Nor am I yet persuaded to put up* in peace what   *accept
200 already I have foolishly suffered.

IAGO   Will you hear me, Roderigo?

RODERIGO   Faith, I have heard too much, and your words and
performances are no kin together.

IAGO   You charge me most unjustly.

205 RODERIGO   With naught but truth. I have wasted myself out of
my means. The jewels you have had from me to deliver to Desdemona
would half have corrupted a votaress.* You have told me she hath   *nun
received them, and returned me expectations and comforts of sudden
respect and acquaintance, but I find none.

210 IAGO   Well, go to! Very well.

RODERIGO   "Very well." "Go to!" I cannot go to, man, nor 'tis not very well! By this hand, I say 'tis very scurvy, and begin to find myself fopped* in it.

deceived

IAGO   Very well.

215 RODERIGO   I tell you 'tis not very well! I will make myself known to Desdemona. If she will return me my jewels, I will give over my suit and repent my unlawful solicitation. If not, assure yourself I will seek satisfaction* of you.

(in a duel)

IAGO   You have said* now.

have spoken

220 RODERIGO   Ay, and said nothing but what I protest intendment of doing.

IAGO   Why, now I see there's mettle in thee, and even from this instant do build on thee a better opinion than ever before. Give me thy hand, Roderigo. Thou hast taken against me a most just exception, but yet I protest I have dealt most directly in thy affair.

225 RODERIGO   It hath not appeared.

IAGO   I grant indeed it hath not appeared, and your suspicion is not without wit and judgment. But, Roderigo, if thou hast that in thee indeed which I have greater reason to believe now than ever—I mean purpose, courage, and valor—this night show it. If thou the next night
230 following enjoy not Desdemona, take me from this world with treachery and devise engines for* my life.

plots against

RODERIGO   Well, what is it? Is it within reason and compass?*

reasonable possibility

IAGO   Sir, there is especial commission come from Venice to depute Cassio in Othello's place.

235 RODERIGO   Is that true? Why, then, Othello and Desdemona return again to Venice.

IAGO   O, no. He goes into Mauritania and takes away with him the fair Desdemona, unless his abode be lingered here by some accident—wherein none can be so determinate* as the removing of Cassio.

effectual

240   RODERIGO   How do you mean, removing him?

IAGO   Why, by making him uncapable of Othello's place: knocking out his brains.

RODERIGO   And that you would have me to do?

IAGO   Ay, if you dare do yourself a profit and a right. He sups tonight
245   with a harlotry,* and thither will I go to him. He knows not yet of his
honorable fortune. If you will watch his going thence (which I will
fashion to fall out* between twelve and one), you may take him at
your pleasure. I will be near to second your attempt, and he shall fall
between us. Come, stand not amazed at it, but go along with me.
250   I will show you such a necessity in his death that you shall think
yourself bound to put it on him. It is now high supper time, and the
night grows to waste. About it!

prostitute

happen

RODERIGO   I will hear further reason for this.

IAGO   And you shall be satisfied.

[*They exit.*]

Scene 3.
Scene continues

[*Enter Othello, Lodovico, Desdemona, Emilia, and Attendants.*]

LODOVICO   I do beseech you, sir, trouble yourself no further.

OTHELLO   O, pardon me, 'twill do me good to walk.

LODOVICO   Madam, good night. I humbly thank your Ladyship.

DESDEMONA   Your Honor is most welcome.

5   OTHELLO   Will you walk, sir?—O, Desdemona—

DESDEMONA   My lord?

OTHELLO   Get you to bed on th' instant. I will be returned forthwith.
Dismiss your attendant there. Look 't be done.

DESDEMONA   I will, my lord.

[*All but Desdemona and Emilia exit.*]

10   EMILIA   How goes it now? He looks gentler than he did.

DESDEMONA   He says he will return incontinent,*   *immediately*
And hath commanded me to go to bed,
And bade me to dismiss you.

EMILIA   Dismiss me?

15   DESDEMONA   It was his bidding. Therefore, good Emilia,
Give me my nightly wearing, and adieu.
We must not now displease him.

EMILIA   I would you had never seen him.

DESDEMONA   So would not I. My love doth so approve him
20 That even his stubbornness, his checks,* his frowns—   *reprimands*
Prithee, unpin me—have grace and favor in them.

EMILIA   I have laid those sheets you bade me on the bed.

DESDEMONA   All's one.* Good faith, how foolish are our minds!   *It doesn't matter*
If I do die before thee, prithee, shroud me
25 In one of those same sheets.

EMILIA   Come, come, you talk!

DESDEMONA   My mother had a maid called Barbary.
She was in love, and he she loved proved mad
And did forsake her. She had a song of willow,
30 An old thing 'twas, but it expressed her fortune,
And she died singing it. That song tonight
Will not go from my mind. I have much to do
But* to go hang my head all at one side   *I can barely restrain myself*
And sing it like poor Barbary. Prithee, dispatch.

35 EMILIA   Shall I go fetch your nightgown?

DESDEMONA   No, unpin me here.
This Lodovico is a proper man.

EMILIA   A very handsome man.

DESDEMONA   He speaks well.

40 EMILIA   I know a lady in Venice would have walked barefoot
to Palestine for a touch of his nether lip.

DESDEMONA   [*singing*] *The poor soul sat sighing by a sycamore tree,*
Sing all a green willow.
Her hand on her bosom, her head on her knee,

Sing willow, willow, willow.
The fresh streams ran by her and murmured her moans,
Sing willow, willow, willow;
Her salt tears fell from her, and softened the stones—
Lay by these.
50 *Sing willow, willow, willow.*
Prithee hie thee!* He'll come anon.   *hurry*
Sing all a green willow must be my garland.
Let nobody blame him, his scorn I approve.
Nay, that's not next. Hark, who is 't that knocks?

55   EMILIA   It's the wind.

DESDEMONA   *I called my love false love, but what said he then?*
Sing willow, willow, willow.
If I court more women, you'll couch with more men.—
So, get thee gone. Good night. Mine eyes do itch;
60 Doth that bode weeping?

EMILIA   'Tis neither here nor there.

DESDEMONA   I have heard it said so. O these men, these men!
Dost thou in conscience think—tell me, Emilia—
That there be women do abuse their husbands
65 In such gross kind?*   *manner (adultery)*

EMILIA   There be some such, no question.

DESDEMONA   Wouldst thou do such a deed for all the world?

EMILIA   Why, would not you?

DESDEMONA   No, by this heavenly light!

70 EMILIA   Nor I neither, by this heavenly light.
I might do 't as well i' th' dark.

DESDEMONA   Wouldst thou do such a deed for all the world?

EMILIA   The world's a huge thing. It is a great price*   *prize
For a small vice.

75   DESDEMONA   In troth, I think thou wouldst not.

EMILIA   In troth, I think I should, and undo 't when I had done it.
Marry,* I would not do such a thing for a joint ring, nor for measures   *Indeed
of lawn,* nor for gowns, petticoats, nor caps, nor any petty exhibition.*   *linen | gift
But for the whole world—'Uds* pity! Who would not make her husband   *God's
80   a cuckold to make him a monarch? I should venture purgatory for 't.

DESDEMONA   Beshrew me if I would do such a wrong for the whole world!

EMILIA   Why, the wrong is but a wrong i' th' world; and, having
the world for your labor, 'tis a wrong in your own world, and you
might quickly make it right.

85   DESDEMONA   I do not think there is any such woman.

EMILIA   Yes, a dozen; and as many to th' vantage* as would   *in addition
store* the world they played for.   *populate
But I do think it is their husbands' faults
If wives do fall. Say that they* slack their duties,   *(husbands)
90   And pour our treasures into foreign laps;
Or else break out in peevish jealousies,
Throwing restraint upon us. Or say they strike us,
Or scant our former having in despite.*   *reduce our allowances out of spite
Why, we have galls,* and though we have some grace,   *tempers
95   Yet have we some revenge. Let husbands know
Their wives have sense like them. They see, and smell,
And have their palates both for sweet and sour,
As husbands have. What is it that they do
When they change us for others? Is it sport?
100   I think it is. And doth affection* breed it?   *lust
I think it doth. Is 't frailty that thus errs?
It is so too. And have not we affections,
Desires for sport, and frailty, as men have?

Then let them use us well. Else let them know,
105 The ills we do, their ills instruct us so.

DESDEMONA   Good night, good night. God me such uses* send,   *habits*
Not to pick bad from bad, but by bad mend.

[*They exit.*]

Act 5.

Scene 1.
A street in Cyprus

[Enter Iago and Roderigo.]

IAGO   Here, stand behind this bulk.* Straight* will he come.   *beam / Immediately*
Wear thy good rapier bare, and put* it home.   *thrust*
Quick, quick! Fear nothing. I'll be at thy elbow.
It makes us or it mars us—think on that,
5   And fix most firm thy resolution.

RODERIGO   Be near at hand. I may miscarry* in 't.   *fail*

IAGO   Here, at thy hand. Be bold and take thy stand.

RODERIGO   I have no great devotion to the deed,
And yet he hath given me satisfying reasons.
10   'Tis but a man gone. Forth, my sword! He dies.
[He draws his sword.]

IAGO   *[aside]* I have rubbed this young quat* almost to the sense,*   *pimple / to the quick*
And he grows angry. Now, whether he kill Cassio,
Or Cassio him, or each do kill the other,
Every way makes my gain. Live Roderigo,*   *If Roderigo lives*
15   He calls me to a restitution large
Of gold and jewels that I bobbed* from him   *took by deception*
As gifts to Desdemona.
It must not be. If Cassio do remain,
He hath a daily beauty in his life
20   That makes me ugly. And besides, the Moor
May unfold* me to him. There stand I in much peril.   *reveal*
No, he must die. Be 't so. I hear him coming.

[Enter Cassio.]

RODERIGO   I know his gait. 'Tis he!—Villain, thou diest!
[*He thrusts at Cassio.*]

CASSIO   That thrust had been mine enemy indeed
25 But that my coat is better* than thou know'st.   *thicker*
I will make proof of* thine.   [*He draws, and stabs Roderigo.*]   *test*

RODERIGO   O, I am slain!   [*Roderigo falls.*]

[*Iago stabs Cassio in the leg, and exits.*]

CASSIO   I am maimed forever! Help, ho! Murder, murder!

[*Enter Othello.*]

OTHELLO   The voice of Cassio! Iago keeps his word.

30 RODERIGO   O, villain that I am!

OTHELLO   [*aside*] It is even so.

CASSIO   O, help ho! Light! A surgeon!

OTHELLO   [*aside*] 'Tis he! O brave Iago, honest and just,
That hast such noble sense of thy friend's wrong!
35 Thou teachest me.—Minion,* your dear lies dead,   *Hussy*
And your unblest fate hies.* Strumpet, I come.   *damnation hurries on*
Forth of my heart those charms, thine eyes, are blotted.
Thy bed, lust-stained, shall with lust's blood be spotted.
[*He exits.*]

[*Enter Lodovico and Gratiano.*]

CASSIO   What ho! No watch?* No passage?* Murder, murder!   *watchmen / passersby*

40 GRATIANO   'Tis some mischance. The voice is very direful.

CASSIO   O, help!

Fight

LODOVICO   Hark!

RODERIGO   O wretched villain!

LODOVICO   Two or three groan. 'Tis heavy night.
45 These may be counterfeits. Let's think 't unsafe
To come in to the cry without more help.

RODERIGO   Nobody come? Then shall I bleed to death.

[*Enter Iago with a light.*]

LODOVICO   Hark!

GRATIANO   Here's one comes in his shirt, with light and weapons.

50 IAGO   Who's there? Whose noise is this that cries on murder?

LODOVICO   We do not know.

IAGO   Did not you hear a cry?

CASSIO   Here, here! For heaven's sake, help me!

IAGO   What's the matter?

55 GRATIANO   [*to Lodovico*] This is Othello's ancient, as I take it.

LODOVICO   The same indeed, a very valiant fellow.

IAGO   [*to Cassio*] What are you here that cry so grievously?

CASSIO   Iago? O, I am spoiled, undone by villains.
Give me some help!

60 IAGO   O me, lieutenant! What villains have done this?

CASSIO   I think that one of them is hereabout
And cannot make* away.   *get*

IAGO   O treacherous villains!
[*To Lodovico and Gratiano*] What are you there?
65   Come in, and give some help.

RODERIGO   O, help me here!

CASSIO   That's one of them.

IAGO   [*to Roderigo*] O murd'rous slave! O villain!
[*He stabs Roderigo.*]

RODERIGO   O damned Iago! O inhuman dog!

70   IAGO   Kill men i' th' dark?—Where be these bloody thieves?
How silent is this town! Ho, murder, murder!—
What may you be? Are you of good or evil?

LODOVICO   As you shall prove us, praise us.

IAGO   Signior Lodovico?

75   LODOVICO   He, sir.

IAGO   I cry you mercy. Here's Cassio hurt by villains.

GRATIANO   Cassio?

IAGO   How is 't, brother?

CASSIO   My leg is cut in two.

80   IAGO   Marry, heaven forbid!
Light, gentlemen. I'll bind it with my shirt.

[*Enter Bianca.*]

BIANCA   What is the matter, ho? Who is 't that cried?

IAGO   Who is 't that cried?

BIANCA   O, my dear Cassio,
85 My sweet Cassio! O Cassio, Cassio, Cassio!

IAGO   O notable strumpet! Cassio, may you suspect
Who they should be that have thus mangled you?

CASSIO   No.

GRATIANO   I am sorry to find you thus; I have been to seek you.

90 IAGO   Lend me a garter. So.—O for a chair
To bear him easily hence!

BIANCA   Alas, he faints. O, Cassio, Cassio, Cassio!

IAGO   Gentlemen all, I do suspect this trash*   (*Bianca*)
To be a party in this injury.—
95 Patience awhile, good Cassio.—Come, come;
Lend me a light. Know we this face or no?
Alas, my friend and my dear countryman
Roderigo? No! Yes, sure. O heaven, Roderigo!

GRATIANO   What, of Venice?

100 IAGO   Even he, sir. Did you know him?

GRATIANO   Know him? Ay.

IAGO   Signior Gratiano? I cry your gentle pardon.
These bloody accidents must excuse my manners
That so neglected you.

105 GRATIANO   I am glad to see you.

IAGO   How do you, Cassio?—O, a chair, a chair!

GRATIANO   Roderigo?

IAGO   He, he, 'tis he! [*A chair is brought in.*] O, that's well said;* the chair.—   *done*
Some good man bear him carefully from hence.
110   I'll fetch the General's surgeon.— [*To Bianca*] For you, mistress,
Save you your labor.—He that lies slain here, Cassio,
Was my dear friend. What malice was between you?

CASSIO   None in the world. Nor do I know the man.

IAGO   [*to Bianca*] What, look you pale?—O, bear him out o' th' air.
[*Cassio, in the chair, and Roderigo are carried off.*]
115   [*To Gratiano and Lodovico*] Stay you, good gentlemen.—
Look you pale, mistress?—
Do you perceive the gastness* of her eye?—   *terror*
Nay, if you stare, we shall hear more anon.—
Behold her well. I pray you, look upon her.
120   Do you see, gentlemen? Nay, guiltiness will speak
Though tongues were out of use.

[*Enter Emilia.*]

EMILIA   Alas, what is the matter? What is the matter, husband?

IAGO   Cassio hath here been set on in the dark
By Roderigo and fellows that are scaped.
125   He's almost slain, and Roderigo dead.

EMILIA   Alas, good gentleman! Alas, good Cassio!

IAGO   This is the fruits of whoring. Prithee, Emilia,
Go know of Cassio where he supped tonight.
[*To Bianca*] What, do you shake at that?

130   BIANCA   He supped at my house, but I therefore shake not.

IAGO   O, did he so? I charge you go with me.

EMILIA   O fie upon thee, strumpet!

BIANCA   I am no strumpet, but of life as honest
As you that thus abuse me.

135   EMILIA   As I? Faugh! Fie upon thee!

IAGO   Kind gentlemen, let's go see poor Cassio dressed.*—   *bandaged*
Come, mistress, you must tell 's another tale.—
Emilia, run you to the citadel
And tell my lord and lady what hath happed.—
140   Will you go on afore? [*Aside*] This is the night
That either makes me or fordoes* me quite.   *undoes*

[*They exit in different directions.*]

Scene 2.
Othello and Desdemona's bedroom

[Enter Othello with a light, and Desdemona in her bed.]

OTHELLO It is the cause, it is the cause,* my soul.   *(of justice)*
Let me not name it to you, you chaste stars.
It is the cause. Yet I'll not shed her blood,
Nor scar that whiter skin of hers than snow,
5 And smooth as monumental alabaster.
Yet she must die, else she'll betray more men.
Put out the light, and then put out the light.
If I quench thee, thou flaming minister,*   *light that serves me*
I can again thy former light restore
10 Should I repent me. But once put out thy light,
Thou cunning'st pattern of excelling nature,*   *artful example of nature's work*
I know not where is that Promethean heat*   *spark of life*
That can thy light relume.* When I have plucked the rose,   *relight*
I cannot give it vital growth again.
15 It needs must wither. I'll smell it on the tree.
O balmy breath, that dost almost persuade
Justice to break her sword! [*He kisses her.*] One more, one more.
Be thus when thou art dead, and I will kill thee
And love thee after. One more, and this the last.   [*He kisses her.*]
20 So sweet was ne'er so fatal. I must weep,
But they are cruel tears. This sorrow's heavenly:
It strikes where it doth love. She wakes.

DESDEMONA Who's there? Othello?

OTHELLO Ay, Desdemona.

25 DESDEMONA Will you come to bed, my lord?

OTHELLO   Have you prayed tonight, Desdemon?

DESDEMONA   Ay, my lord.

OTHELLO   If you bethink yourself of any crime
Unreconciled as yet to heaven and grace,
30 Solicit* for it straight.   *Ask forgiveness*

DESDEMONA   Alack, my lord,
What may you mean by that?

OTHELLO   Well, do it, and be brief. I will walk by.
I would not kill thy unpreparèd spirit.
35 No, heaven forfend!* I would not kill thy soul.   *forbid*

DESDEMONA   Talk you of killing?

OTHELLO   Ay, I do.

DESDEMONA   Then heaven have mercy on me.

OTHELLO   Amen, with all my heart.

40 DESDEMONA   If you say so, I hope you will not kill me.

OTHELLO   Humh.

DESDEMONA   And yet I fear you, for you're fatal then
When your eyes roll so. Why I should fear I know not,
Since guiltiness I know not, but yet I feel I fear.

45 OTHELLO   Think on thy sins.

DESDEMONA   They are loves I bear to you.

OTHELLO   Ay, and for that thou diest.

DESDEMONA   That death's unnatural that kills for loving.
Alas, why gnaw you so your nether lip?

50   Some bloody passion shakes your very frame.
These are portents, but yet I hope, I hope
They do not point on me.

OTHELLO   Peace, and be still.

DESDEMONA   I will so. What's the matter?

55   OTHELLO   That handkerchief
Which I so loved, and gave thee, thou gav'st to Cassio.

DESDEMONA   No, by my life and soul! Send for the man
And ask him.

OTHELLO   Sweet soul, take heed, take heed of perjury.
60   Thou art on thy deathbed.

DESDEMONA   Ay, but not yet to die.

OTHELLO   Yes, presently.*   *immediately
Therefore confess thee freely of thy sin.
For to deny each article with oath
65   Cannot remove nor choke the strong conception
That I do groan withal. Thou art to die.

DESDEMONA   Then Lord have mercy on me!

OTHELLO   I say "Amen."

DESDEMONA   And have you mercy, too. I never did
70   Offend you in my life, never loved Cassio
But with such general warranty of heaven
As I might love. I never gave him token.

OTHELLO   By heaven, I saw my handkerchief in 's hand!
O perjured woman, thou dost stone* my heart   *harden
75   And mak'st me call what I intend to do
A murder, which I thought a sacrifice!
I saw the handkerchief!

DESDEMONA   He found it, then.
I never gave it him. Send for him hither.
Let him confess a truth.

OTHELLO   He hath confessed.

DESDEMONA   What, my lord?

OTHELLO   That he hath used thee.

DESDEMONA   How? Unlawfully?

OTHELLO   Ay.

DESDEMONA   He will not say so.

OTHELLO   No. His mouth is stopped.
Honest Iago hath ta'en order for 't.

DESDEMONA   O, my fear interprets. What, is he dead?

OTHELLO   Had all his hairs been lives, my great revenge
Had stomach for them all.

DESDEMONA   Alas, he is betrayed, and I undone.   [*She weeps.*]

OTHELLO   Out, strumpet! Weep'st thou for him to my face?

DESDEMONA   O banish me, my lord, but kill me not!

OTHELLO   Down, strumpet!

DESDEMONA   Kill me tomorrow, let me live tonight.

OTHELLO   Nay, if you strive—

DESDEMONA   But half an hour!

OTHELLO   Being done, there is no pause.

100   DESDEMONA   But while I say one prayer!

OTHELLO   It is too late.   [*He smothers her.*]

EMILIA   [*within*] My lord, my lord? What ho! My lord, my lord!

OTHELLO   What noise is this?—Not dead? Not yet quite dead?
I that am cruel am yet merciful.
105   I would not have thee linger in thy pain.
So, so.

EMILIA   [*within*] What, ho! My lord, my lord!

OTHELLO   Who's there?

EMILIA   [*within*] O, good my lord, I would speak a word with you.

110   OTHELLO   Yes. 'Tis Emilia.—By and by.—She's dead.
'Tis like* she comes to speak of Cassio's death.   *likely*
The noise was here. Ha, no more moving?
Still as the grave. Shall she come in? Were 't good?
I think she stirs again. No. What's best to do?
115   If she come in, she'll sure speak to my wife.
My wife, my wife! What wife? I have no wife.
O insupportable! O heavy hour!
Methinks it should be now a huge eclipse
Of sun and moon, and that th' affrighted globe
120   Should yawn at alteration.*   *gape at this change*

EMILIA   [*within*] I do beseech you
That I may speak with you. O, good my lord—

OTHELLO   I had forgot thee. O, come in, Emilia.—
Soft,* by and by, let me the curtains* draw.—   *Quiet | bed curtains*
125   Where art thou?
[*Enter Emilia.*]
                    What's the matter with thee now?

EMILIA   O, my good lord, yonder's foul murders done.

OTHELLO   What? Now?

EMILIA   But* now, my lord.   *Just

130   OTHELLO   It is the very error* of the moon.   *deviation
She comes more nearer Earth than she was wont
And makes men mad.

EMILIA   Cassio, my lord, hath killed
A young Venetian called Roderigo.

135   OTHELLO   Roderigo killed? And Cassio killed?

EMILIA   No, Cassio is not killed.

OTHELLO   Not Cassio killed? Then murder's out of tune,
And sweet revenge grows harsh.

DESDEMONA   O falsely, falsely murdered.

140   EMILIA   O Lord, what cry is that?

OTHELLO   That? What?

EMILIA   Out, and alas, that was my lady's voice!
Help! Help ho! Help! O lady, speak again!
Sweet Desdemona, O sweet mistress, speak!

145   DESDEMONA   A guiltless death I die.

EMILIA   O, who hath done this deed?

DESDEMONA   Nobody. I myself. Farewell.
Commend me to my kind lord. O, farewell.   [*She dies.*]

OTHELLO   Why, how should she be murdered?

150 EMILIA   Alas, who knows?

OTHELLO   You heard her say herself, it was not I.

EMILIA   She said so. I must needs report the truth.

OTHELLO   She's like a liar gone to burning hell!
'Twas I that killed her.

155 EMILIA   O, the more angel she, and you the blacker devil!

OTHELLO   She turned to folly,* and she was a whore.   *wantonness

EMILIA   Thou dost belie* her, and thou art a devil!   *tell lies about

OTHELLO   She was false as water.

EMILIA   Thou art rash as fire to say
160 That she was false. O, she was heavenly true!

OTHELLO   Cassio did top her. Ask thy husband else.*   *if you doubt it
O, I were damned beneath all depth in hell
But that I did proceed upon just grounds
To this extremity. Thy husband knew it all.

165 EMILIA   My husband?

OTHELLO   Thy husband.

EMILIA   That she was false to wedlock?

OTHELLO   Ay, with Cassio. Had she been true,
If heaven would make me such another world
170 Of one entire and perfect chrysolite,
I'd not have sold her for it.

EMILIA   My husband?

OTHELLO   Ay, 'twas he that told me on her first.
An honest man he is, and hates the slime
175 That sticks on filthy deeds.

EMILIA   My husband?

OTHELLO   What needs this iterance,* woman? I say, thy husband.   *repetition*

EMILIA   O mistress, villainy hath made mocks with* love!—   *mockery of*
My husband say she was false?

180 OTHELLO   He, woman.
I say thy husband. Dost understand the word?
My friend, thy husband; honest, honest Iago.

EMILIA   If he say so, may his pernicious soul
Rot half a grain a day! He lies to th' heart!
185 She was too fond of her most filthy bargain.

OTHELLO   Hah?

EMILIA   Do thy worst!
This deed of thine is no more worthy heaven
Than thou wast worthy her.

190 OTHELLO   Peace, you were best!*   *It would be best for you to be silent*

EMILIA   Thou hast not half that power to do me harm
As I have to be hurt. O gull!* O dolt,   *fool*
As ignorant as dirt! Thou hast done a deed—
I care not for thy sword. I'll make thee known,
195 Though I lost twenty lives. Help! Help, ho! Help!
The Moor hath killed my mistress! Murder, murder!

[*Enter Montano, Gratiano, and Iago.*]

MONTANO   What is the matter? How now, general?

EMILIA   O, are you come, Iago? You have done well,
That men must lay their murders on your neck.

200   GRATIANO   What is the matter?

EMILIA   [to Iago] Disprove this villain, if thou be'st a man.
He says thou told'st him that his wife was false.
I know thou didst not. Thou 'rt not such a villain.
Speak, for my heart is full.

205   IAGO   I told him what I thought, and told no more
Than what he found himself was apt and true.

EMILIA   But did you ever tell him she was false?

IAGO   I did.

EMILIA   You told a lie, an odious, damnèd lie!
210   Upon my soul, a lie, a wicked lie!
She false with Cassio? Did you say with Cassio?

IAGO   With Cassio, mistress. Go to! Charm* your tongue.   *Silence*

EMILIA   I will not charm my tongue. I am bound to speak.
My mistress here lies murdered in her bed.

215   ALL   O heavens forfend!*   *forbid*

EMILIA   [to Iago] And your reports have set the murder on!

OTHELLO   Nay, stare not, masters; it is true indeed.

GRATIANO   'Tis a strange truth.

MONTANO   O monstrous act!

220   EMILIA   Villainy, villainy, villainy!
I think upon 't, I think! I smell 't! O villainy!

Discovery

I thought so then. I'll kill myself for grief!
O villainy! Villainy!

IAGO   What, are you mad? I charge you get you home.

225   EMILIA   Good gentlemen, let me have leave to speak.
'Tis proper I obey him, but not now.
Perchance, Iago, I will ne'er go home.

OTHELLO   O, O, O!   [*He falls on the bed.*]

EMILIA   Nay, lay thee down, and roar!
230   For thou hast killed the sweetest innocent
That e'er did lift up eye.

OTHELLO   [*standing*] O, she was foul!—
I scarce did know you, uncle.* There lies your niece,   *(Gratiano, Brabantio's brother)*
Whose breath indeed these hands have newly stopped.
235   I know this act shows* horrible and grim.   *looks*

GRATIANO   Poor Desdemon, I am glad thy father's dead.
Thy match was mortal to him, and pure grief
Shore his old thread in twain.* Did he live now,   *cut the thread of his life*
This sight would make him do a desperate turn,*   *deed*
240   Yea, curse his better angel* from his side,   *guardian angel*
And fall to reprobance.*   *damnation*

OTHELLO   'Tis pitiful. But yet Iago knows
That she with Cassio hath the act of shame
A thousand times committed. Cassio confessed it,
245   And she did gratify his amorous works
With that recognizance* and pledge of love   *token*
Which I first gave her. I saw it in his hand.
It was a handkerchief, an antique token
My father gave my mother.

250   EMILIA   O God! O heavenly God!

IAGO   Zounds, hold your peace!

EMILIA   'Twill out, 'twill out. I peace?
No, I will speak as liberal as the north.*   *freely as the north wind*
Let heaven and men and devils, let them all,
255   All, all, cry shame against me, yet I'll speak.

IAGO   Be wise, and get you home.   [*He draws his sword.*]

EMILIA   I will not.

GRATIANO   Fie, your sword upon a woman!

EMILIA   O thou dull Moor, that handkerchief thou speak'st of
260   I found by fortune, and did give my husband—
For often, with a solemn earnestness
(More than indeed belonged to such a trifle),
He begged of me to steal 't.

IAGO   Villainous whore!

265   EMILIA   She give it Cassio? No, alas, I found it,
And I did give 't my husband.

IAGO   Filth, thou liest!

EMILIA   By heaven, I do not, I do not, gentlemen!
[*To Othello*] O murd'rous coxcomb,* what should such a fool   *fool*
270   Do with so good a wife?

OTHELLO   Are there no stones* in heaven   *thunderbolts*
But what serves for the thunder?—Precious* villain!   *Complete*

[*The Moor runs at Iago but is disarmed.*
Iago kills his wife.]

GRATIANO   The woman falls! Sure he hath killed his wife.

EMILIA   Ay, ay! O, lay me by my mistress' side.

[*Iago exits.*]

275   GRATIANO   He's gone, but his wife's killed.

MONTANO   'Tis a notorious villain. Take you this weapon
Which I have here recovered from the Moor.
Come, guard the door without. Let him not pass,
But kill him rather. I'll after that same villain,
280   For 'tis a damnèd slave.

[*Montano and Gratiano exit.*]

OTHELLO   I am not valiant neither,
But every puny whipster* gets my sword.   *slight person*
But why should honor outlive honesty?
Let it go all.

285   EMILIA   What did thy song bode,* lady?   *portend*
Hark, canst thou hear me? I will play the swan
And die in music.
[*She sings.*] *Willow, willow, willow.*
Moor, she was chaste. She loved thee, cruel Moor.
290   So come my soul to bliss, as I speak true.
So speaking as I think, alas, I die.   [*She dies.*]

OTHELLO   I have another weapon in this chamber.
It is a sword of Spain, the ice brook's temper.*   *tempered in ice-cold water*
O, here it is.—Uncle, I must come forth.

295   GRATIANO   [*within*] If thou attempt it, it will cost thee dear;
Thou hast no weapon and perforce must suffer.

OTHELLO   Look in upon me, then, and speak with me,
Or naked* as I am I will assault thee.   *unarmed*

[*Enter Gratiano.*]

GRATIANO   What is the matter?

300 OTHELLO   Behold, I have a weapon.
A better never did itself sustain
Upon a soldier's thigh. I have seen the day
That with this little arm and this good sword
I have made my way through more impediments
305 Than twenty times your stop.* But—O vain boast!—   *power to stop*
Who can control his fate? 'Tis not so now.
Be not afraid, though you do see me weaponed.
Here is my journey's end, here is my butt*   *end point*
And very sea-mark* of my utmost sail.*   *beacon | journey's limit*
310 Do you go back dismayed? 'Tis a lost* fear.   *unnecessary*
Man but a rush against Othello's breast,
And he retires. Where should Othello go?
[*He looks toward the bed.*]
Now, how dost thou look now? O ill-starred wench,
Pale as thy smock, when we shall meet at compt,*   *Judgment Day*
315 This look of thine will hurl my soul from heaven,
And fiends will snatch at it. Cold, cold, my girl?
Even like thy chastity.—O cursèd, cursèd slave!—
Whip me, you devils,
From the possession of this heavenly sight!
320 Blow me about in winds, roast me in sulfur,
Wash me in steep-down gulfs of liquid fire!
O Desdemon! Dead, Desdemon! Dead! O, O!

[*Enter Lodovico, Cassio in a chair, Montano, and Iago, with Officers.*]

LODOVICO   Where is this rash and most unfortunate man?

OTHELLO   That's he that was Othello. Here I am.

325 LODOVICO   Where is that viper? Bring the villain forth.

[*Iago is brought forward.*]

OTHELLO   I look down towards his feet; but that's a fable.—
If that thou be'st a devil, I cannot kill thee.   [*He stabs Iago.*]

LODOVICO   Wrench his sword from him.

[*Othello is disarmed.*]

IAGO   I bleed, sir, but not killed.

330   OTHELLO   I am not sorry neither. I'd have thee live,
For in my sense* 'tis happiness to die.   *emotional state*

LODOVICO   O thou Othello, that wert once so good,
Fall'n in the practice* of a damnèd slave,   *deception*
What shall be said to thee?

335   OTHELLO   Why, anything.
An honorable murderer, if you will,
For naught I did in hate, but all in honor.

LODOVICO   This wretch hath part confessed his villainy.
Did you and he consent in Cassio's death?

340   OTHELLO   Ay.

CASSIO   Dear general, I never gave you cause.

OTHELLO   I do believe it, and I ask your pardon.
Will you, I pray, demand that demi-devil
Why he hath thus ensnared my soul and body?

345   IAGO   Demand me nothing. What you know, you know.
From this time forth I never will speak word.

LODOVICO   What? Not to pray?

GRATIANO   Torments* will ope your lips.   *Torture*

OTHELLO   Well, thou dost best.

LODOVICO   Sir,
You shall understand what hath befall'n,
Which, as I think, you know not. Here is a letter
Found in the pocket of the slain Roderigo,
And here another. [*He shows papers.*] The one of them imports
The death of Cassio, to be undertook
By Roderigo.

OTHELLO   O villain!

CASSIO   Most heathenish and most gross.*   *flagrant*

LODOVICO   Now here's another discontented paper*   *letter listing discontents*
Found in his pocket, too; and this it seems
Roderigo meant t' have sent this damnèd villain,
But that, belike,* Iago in the interim   *probably*
Came in and satisfied him.

OTHELLO   O, thou pernicious caitiff!*—   *wretch*
How came you, Cassio, by that handkerchief
That was my wife's?

CASSIO   I found it in my chamber.
And he himself confessed it but even now,
That there he dropped it for a special purpose
Which wrought to his desire.

OTHELLO   O fool, fool, fool!

CASSIO   There is besides, in Roderigo's letter,
How he upbraids Iago, that he made him
Brave* me upon the watch, whereon it came   *Defy*
That I was cast.* And even but now he spake,   *dismissed*
After long seeming dead: Iago hurt him,
Iago set him on.

LODOVICO   [*to Othello*] You must forsake this room and go with us.
Your power and your command is taken off,

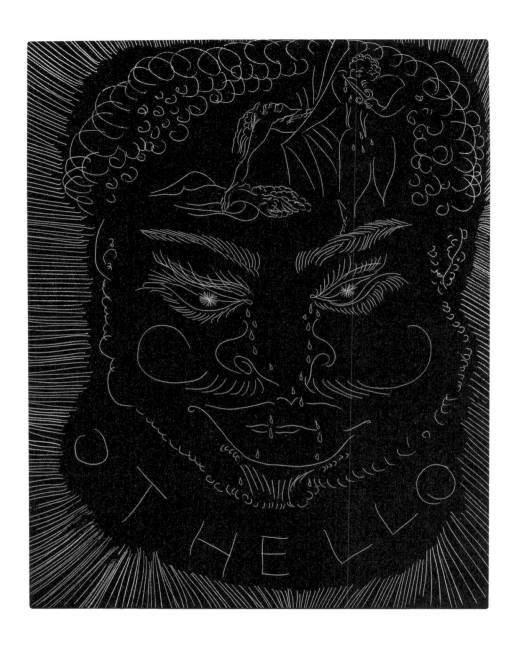

380 And Cassio rules in Cyprus. For this slave,
If there be any cunning cruelty
That can torment him much and hold him* long, *(alive)*
It shall be his. You shall close* prisoner rest, *remain a closely guarded*
Till that the nature of your fault be known
385 To the Venetian state.—Come, bring away.

OTHELLO   Soft you.* A word or two before you go. *Wait*
I have done the state some service, and they know 't.
No more of that. I pray you in your letters,
When you shall these unlucky* deeds relate, *unfortunate*
390 Speak of me as I am. Nothing extenuate,
Nor set down aught in malice. Then must you speak
Of one that loved not wisely, but too well;
Of one not easily jealous, but being wrought,
Perplexed in the extreme; of one whose hand,
395 Like the base Judean, threw a pearl away
Richer than all his tribe; of one whose subdued* eyes, *(by tears)*
Albeit unused to the melting mood,
Drops tears as fast as the Arabian trees
Their medicinable gum. Set you down this.
400 And say besides, that in Aleppo once,
Where a malignant* and a turbanned Turk *evil*
Beat a Venetian and traduced the state,
I took by th' throat the circumcisèd dog,
And smote him, thus.   [*He stabs himself.*]

405 LODOVICO   O bloody period!* *conclusion*

GRATIANO   All that is spoke is marred.

OTHELLO   [*to Desdemona*] I kissed thee ere I killed thee. No way but this,
Killing myself, to die upon a kiss.   [*He dies.*]

CASSIO   This did I fear, but thought he had no weapon,
410 For he was great of heart.

LODOVICO   [*to Iago*] O Spartan* dog,   *cruel*
      More fell than anguish, hunger, or the sea,
      Look on the tragic loading of this bed.
      This is thy work.—The object poisons sight.
415   Let it be hid.—Gratiano, keep* the house,   *guard*
      And seize upon the fortunes of the Moor,
      For they succeed on you. [*To Cassio*] To you, lord governor,
      Remains the censure* of this hellish villain.   *sentence*
      The time, the place, the torture, O, enforce it.
420   Myself will straight aboard, and to the state
      This heavy act with heavy heart relate.

      [*They exit.*]

Othello
William Shakespeare × Chris Ofili

From the series *Seeing Shakespeare*

David Zwirner Books
529 West 20th Street, 2nd Floor
New York, New York 10011
+1 212 727 2070
davidzwirnerbooks.com

Managing Director Doro Globus
Editorial Director Lucas Zwirner

Project Editor Elizabeth Gordon
Proofreader Dorothy Feaver

Design Sarah Schrauwen
Production Manager Jules Thomson
Production Assistant Liz Koehler
Color Separations VeronaLibri, Verona
Printing VeronaLibri, Verona

Typeface Freight Text
Paper Multi Offset, 120 gsm

Publication © 2019 David Zwirner Books
"Ofili's Othello" © 2019 Fred Moten
Artwork © 2019 Chris Ofili

Photography p. 1: Kerry McFate;
pp. 35, 40, 59, 64, 90, 101, 145, 156, 161,
168, 173: courtesy Two Palms, New York

Distributed in the United States
and Canada by
Simon & Schuster, Inc.
1230 Avenue of the Americas
New York, New York 10020
simonandschuster.com

Distributed outside the United States
and Canada by
Thames & Hudson, Ltd.
181A High Holborn
London WC1V 7QX
thamesandhudson.com

ISBN 978-1-64423-022-0
Library of Congress Control Number:
2019909861

Printed in Italy

Frontispiece p.1: Chris Ofili, *Othello*,
2019. Oil on linen, $19^{5}/_{8} \times 15^{5}/_{8}$ inches
(49.8×39.7 cm)

Works pp. 35, 40, 59, 64, 90, 101, 145, 156,
161, 168, 173: Chris Ofili, *Othello*, 2018.
Portfolio of ten etchings with title page
and colophon. Aquatint, black mica, and
white ink on En Tout Cas paper. Each,
$14^{7}/_{8} \times 11^{1}/_{4}$ inches (37.8×28.6 cm)

Cover Chris Ofili, *Jealousy* (detail),
from *Othello*, 2018

David Zwirner wishes to thank
Chris Ofili, without whom this edition,
the first in David Zwirner Books's
Seeing Shakespeare series, would not have
been possible. Special thanks are also
due to Fred Moten for his illuminating
text and to Two Palms, New York.